The whole BIBLE in a year for HIGH-SCHOOL

50 LESSONS
FROM GENESIS TO REVELATION!

e625.com
The whole Bible in a year for High School
Howard Andruejol, Willy Gómez
Originally published in Spanish
Published by e625® © 2024
Dallas, Texas
United States of America

ISBN: 978-1-954149-54-0

© 2006, 2008 by Sociedad Bíblica Internacional
Used with permit. All rights reserved.

Unless indicated otherwise, Scripture quotations are taken from the Holy Bible, NEW INTERNATIONAL VERSION®.
© 1973, 1978, 1984 by Biblica Inc. All rights reserved worldwide. Used by permission.

Translated by: David Ortíz
Disgned by: Creatorstudio.net

TABLE OF CONTENTS

Introduction to the Series..5

Introduction..9

Lesson 1 > Starting...11

Lesson 2 > Genesis...14

Lesson 3 > Exodus and Leviticus.................................19

Lesson 4 > Numbers and Deuteronomy.....................23

Lesson 5 > Joshua..28

Lesson 6 > Judges..32

Lesson 7 > 1 and 2 Samuel..37

Lesson 8 > 1 and 2 Kings...42

Lesson 9 > Job..44

Lesson 10 > Psalms..49

Lesson 11 > Proverbs...52

Lesson 12 > Ecclesiastes and Song of Songs............55

Lesson 13 > Obadiah and Joel.....................................60

Lesson 14 > Hosea and Amos......................................64

Lesson 15 > Isaiah..68

Lesson 16 > Nahum, Habakkuk and Zephaniah.........70

Lesson 17 > Ezekiel and Daniel....................................75

Lesson 18 > Jeremiah and Lamentations...................79

Lesson 19 > Haggai and Zechariah.............................83

Lesson 20 > Esther...87

Lesson 21 > Ezra and Nehemiah..................................91

Lesson 22 > Malachi...97

Lesson 23 > How are the OT and NT different but complementary?..101

Lesson 24 > The Gospels: Mark..................................104

Lesson 25 > The Gospels: Luke..................................109

Lesson 26 > The Gospels: Matthew............................115

Lesson 27 > The Gospels: John..................................119

Lesson 28 > Acts 1-12...123

Lesson 29 > Acts 13-28...127

Lesson 30 > James..129

Lesson 31 > Galatians...133

Lesson 32 > 1 and 2 Thessalonians.............................138

Lesson 33 > 1 Corinthians..142

Lesson 34 > 2 Corinthians..147

Lesson 35 > Romans (Part 1).......................................151

Lesson 36 > Romans (Part 2)......................................155

Lesson 37 > Ephesians...158

Lesson 38 > Philippians..162

Lesson 39 > Colossians..166

Lesson 40 > Philemon...170

Lesson 41 > 1 Timothy and Titus.................................174

Lesson 42 > 2 Timothy..179

Lesson 43 > 1 Peter...183

Lesson 44 > 2 Peter..187

Lesson 45 > Jude...191

Lesson 46 > Hebrews..194

Lesson 47 > 1 John..198

Lesson 48 > 2 and 3 John..203

Lesson 49 > Revelation...207

Lesson 50 > What does God want us to do with our knowledge of the Bible?..................................212

INTRODUCTION TO THE SERIES
"All Scripture is inspired by God and is profitable."

2 Timothy 3:16 (CSB)

We are very happy to bring you this series of lessons from the whole Bible. Studing this series will take you on a fascinating tour of a library that consists of sixty-six volumes, which allows you to get to know God's character, his perfect work, and his wonderful expectations toward us.

Today, many churches have developed the harmful habit of reading the biblical texts in small fragments. If you pay attention, you'll notice how in classes, small groups, preaching, devotionals, and daily reading planners, it has become common practice to read isolated portions of the Bible. This is not necessarily wrong, but if we develop the habit of reading it only in this manner, we run the risk of taking the loose texts as snacks, or even as if they were phrases of the horoscope. On the other hand, to delve deeper into the complete story and take the time to notice its details and its applications, will help us to ensure that later on we will have a better understanding of those loose texts.

Try this exercise: Ask 10 Christians, of any age, something as simple as "What is the Bible about?" and you will get 12 different answers. Ask them to explain to you how the Old and New Testaments relate, and possibly some will begin to hesitate. If you want to go a bit further, ask them to explain to you what the book of Obadiah is about, and how it relates to the rest of the Bible and to us today.

These should not be questions that only seminarians or pastors are able to answer. All believers need to be able to answer them, and that is why this material is so important.

The reason for this is very simple. Imagine for a moment a jigsaw puzzle, one that's difficult to put together. Would it have a thousand pieces? A thousand five hundred? Let's imagine one that has two thousand pieces, and let's try the following experiment. Imagine now that I take the puzzle box, and hide the cover that contains the image that must be put together. Then I will ask you to put in your hand randomly, and take out only ten pieces.

Now comes the interesting part. What if I asked you to describe the image? Do you think you'd be able to do it? Of course not! You could make something up, but you certainly would not be able to guess the whole image.

At many churches throughout the continent we asked the same question. What are the most famous biblical texts that all churches know? At every city where we tried this exercise, the response was always the same ten verses.

Yes, just ten verses. It appears that our new generations are growing up with only 10 of the 31,130 pieces of the biblical puzzle. And with those ten verses, we expect them to have a clear picture of God's character, his perfect work, and his expectation toward us. It's an impossible request. They will undoubtedly develop an image that's false, incomplete, distorted, and disfigured.

Just as it is important to appreciate the fine detail of each piece of the puzzle, it is also indispensable to be able to see the complete picture. And that's what these lessons are about.

We have prepared this manual as much as possible as a chronological journey through God's revelation, from Genesis through Revelation. It is our hope that, having an overview of the biblical books, your students will react in two ways.

First, that they'll be able to say, "Now I understand what this book is about!" Each lesson will be effective to the extent that each participant is able to have a better understanding of the content and purpose of the books of the Bible.

As you will see, since this adventure is designed for a full year of lessons, it is not possible to include all 66 books in just 50 lessons. It has been a difficult decision to compress, summarize, or omit. Moreover, we are convinced that Genesis on its own should take us through 50 weeks! We are confident that we are building a solid foundation, and that we will continue to build on it with more in-depth studies of the specific books. We are looking forward to what will follow from this.

Second, that by understanding better the full picture, they will now be motivated to learn more about the details. If they are able to connect each book of the Bible to the complete image of the puzzle, each individual chapter will make more sense. We want to develop devout readers of the biblical text, scholars of God's Word. Join them on this tour, help them to explore the richness of each individual biblical passage. Take the time to dig deep into specific books of the Bible, as well as complete biographies of biblical characters.

INTRODUCTION TO THE SERIES

In addition to considering the maturity and contextual characteristics of each age group, we have chosen to approach this series through a lens with which to look at the biblical books. With it we underline the great theological and anthropological themes of the Bible.

Each volume is unique and complementary. Those who travel with us through these four books will certainly have a clear idea of what the Bible is about!

The children's volume was developed around an identity that's outside of this world. The biblical journey will focus on the progressive revelation of God's character. Who is he? How does he present himself to humans? Knowing God allows us also know our own identity: What is our natural condition? How is this identity manifested in our behavior? We need to be rescued from this condition, with Jesus Christ being our only hope. To receive him as Lord and Savior renews us. Who are we now in Christ? How does this transformation manifest itself in our behavior?

The volume for preadolescents focuses on an unconditional and eternal relationship. The biblical journey will focus on God's initiative to relate to humans. It will highlight the invincible obstacle for man-sin, and Christ's complete victory. The emphasis is on God's faithfulness to man–despite our infidelity–and the closeness that it allows us, only through Christ. What defines God's relationship with us? What should I do to live that relationship today?

The volume for high school focuses on crucial decisions. The biblical journey will focus on God's expectations, given our new identity, of lives lived according to his character. We will study the divine perspective in order to make the right decisions in every facet of our lives, the purpose of holiness, and the dire consequences of disobedience. The Gospel is not focused on our behavior, but given the grace of God, our best response is to glorify him.

The volume for university students is mission focused. The biblical journey will focus on God's mission, which seeks to redeem human beings. Special attention will be paid to how God has at all times fulfilled and will continue to fulfill until the end his plan for human beings. Salvation is available to anyone. Our new identity sends us to explain this Gospel to every person, even to the most remote places on the planet. This is our true life purpose, to live in mission here and there, now.

On our website, www.e625.com, you will find supplementary material for our lessons. Our goal for the conversations that arise in each lesson is that they be theologically deep and didactically creative.

Of course, all this has been the work of a great team of people involved in the design of the curriculum and instruction. Upon hearing the idea, many friends enthusiastically joined this project.

To each of you, thank you for investing in the biblical formation of our new generations!

Let's lead them to know the whole puzzle, to have a biblical image of the person of God, to understand his eternal plan, and the response he expects from each one of us.

Let's learn together!

Howard Andruejol and Lucas Leys
general editors

INDEX OF SYMBOLS

 Questions to ask the group or one of the participants in particular

 Group dynamics to strengthen concepts and teamwork and encourage participation

 Notes just for you!

 Visit the website e625.com/lessons to obtain additional materials

INTRODUCTION

Don't let the trees prevent you from seeing the forest.

This is what we want. Sometimes we teach the Bible to adolescents in fragments: a verse here, a passage there, but we don't show them the context. That is not necessarily wrong, but we believe it is important to give an overview of each of the books in the Bible so that the meaning of the message that each book intends to convey, as well as that of the Bible as a whole, is not lost.

This tool that you have in your hands will help you present the books of the Bible to your group of teens. In its pages you will find dynamics, notes for you, questions for the group, and other resources, to prepare your session of one hour a week with them. We did not intent for this work to be exhaustive, but we did strive to be pedagogical and challenging. The Bible is not a book to be read as you would a newspaper, but rather to be studied in depth, and above all to be assimilated, digested. The Bible invites us to "feed" on the Word!

We propose a general perspective of the Bible with some important texts and stories, and also some that are not as well known. Our hope is that, with your help, adolescents will delve further into Scripture on their own. It would be great if at this time of their lives they developed a vivid and constant relationship with God and his Word. It is a time when they must make crucial decisions for their future, and we hope to be useful in that regard.

Therefore, they will have five devotionals a week that they can complete by reading a biblical text and answering some questions. This will help them to strengthen their learning experience and to apply it in a practical way to their daily lives.

Of course, this material is fully connected to the page e625.com/lessons, from which you can download all the additional resources necessary for you to continue with your discipleship project to the new generations.

Thank you for your continued belief that God transforms hearts, regardless of age. We know that your work is not in vain.

50 lessons methodology

We want to introduce for your sessions a constructivist work methodology. What does that mean?

Ideally, the participation of the adolescents will define the session. If they take part, if they discover for themselves the truths of each book of the Bible, they will remember it much better than if you simply teach them a lesson. The idea is to build each lesson together, so that they can be active participants and share their concerns with you and with each other.

You will be the main voice, and you will facilitate the learning process. You will introduce and explain the material, but you will seek everyone's participation. It's great if they can approach Scripture on their own and discover its truths for their lives!

This book is for you so make it your own. You should spend at least one hour to prepare for each session. You must not say everything just as it is written. Dare to adapt it to your own context. Let us be constructivists from the beginning! Underline, add what you consider important, pray, prepare the downloads of e625.com/lessons, have videos and dynamics ready for adolescents to participate.

The more you master the lesson, the freer you will feel to ensure that everyone can take part, and that is what it's all about. It would be great in this context if a spirit of community develops, so that adolescents arrive with a desire to meet together again in order to discover and interpret the Bible together.

Lesson 1 > STARTING
Why is studying the entire Bible important?

In the first session it is important that the members of the group get to know each other, as this is essential for everyone to be able to participate. To do this, we will ask questions and propose some dynamics during your time together. Remember that the objective is that they become passionate about the Word of God and grow together with their companions in a living relationship with Jesus. Be cheerful! Try to generate freedom in the participations, but remember the pedagogical objectives of each session, and try to follow the guidelines while being sensitive to the needs of your adolescents.

Again, we invite you to read the lesson in advance, underline the most significant items, and write-in and add those things that you want to include from your own experience and personal study in order to inspire them. The most important thing is to assimilate the concepts and handle them naturally. The Bible continues to transform lives!

Download complementary material for this section at www.e625.com/lessons.

Bible, from the Greek biblos ("books" or "small books"), is not a book: It is many! It is a unique collection that tells the story of God with His people, made of flesh and blood, who made good and bad decisions, as well as serious mistakes, but who also allowed themselves to be guided by God. There is history, poetry, creativity, battles, and love stories. There is no book in history reproduced more or translated into more languages than the Bible. Many have given their lives in past centuries and the present one, so that we may be able to have the joy of studying the Bible today. Let's not waste this opportunity.

Do you know some of these stories and characters? What bad decisions did they make? What were the consequences? Why do you think these stories are in the Bible?

Division and structure of the Bible
The Bible has sixty-six books that are divided into two large collections.

The Old Testament, with thirty-nine books, occupies the first part of the Bible and tells the story from the origins of creation, through the early history of the people of Israel, their dispersion and their return to the promised land, until approximately 400

BC (before Christ). It contains historical books with subjects such as law, wisdom (practical advice) and poetry, as well as books of prophesy.

The New Testament consists of twenty-seven books that tells the story of the birth of Jesus; his life, death, and resurrection; and the consequences this had during the early years of the church when his message spread from Jerusalem to the heart of the Roman Empire. In it we find letters (this is what the word *epistle* means), history, the four Gospels, and the book of Revelation.

Although it is a very diverse book, written by many authors from different cultures and eras over many centuries of writing, the Bible makes complete sense and tells the story of how God created human beings to be free, to make our own decisions, and to be responsible for our own lives.

We made wrong decisions, and it had consequences. God took the initiative to save us from our bad actions by teaching us and giving us the ability to make good decisions again. The Bible tells us about this, over and over.

During these sessions we will go over many examples in order to learn how to become part of this story that's in the Bible, since it's also the story of each one of us.

What's your favorite book in the Bible? Why?

Let them talk freely and be ready to share your answer.

Once the dynamics are set, we ask them:

Why do you think the Bible has options?

When we make decisions we take many things into account: our interest, if it will be good for us or for others, if in the future we will regret having done it, if it is what our parents want us to do, if it will make us feel happier, or how has that decision worked out for us in the past. What is the best way of making good decisions? Look at what Paul, one of the authors of the Bible, says in the last letter he wrote, in his living testament: 2 Timothy 3:14–17.

Have teens brought their Bibles or apps? Have them search for it themselves.

> *But as for you, continue in what you have learned and have become convinced of, because you know those from whom you learned it, and how from infancy you have known the Holy Scriptures, which are able to make you wise for salvation through*

faith in Christ Jesus. All Scripture is God-breathed and is useful for teaching, rebuking, correcting and training in righteousness, so that the servant of God may be thoroughly equipped for every good work.

❓ What is the the Bible useful for, according to this text?

❓ How do you think the Bible is useful for you today, in your own life?

The Bible is called the Word of God, and it helps us see life from his perspective. That is why it is important that we study it. Through it we can be saved and we can learn how to live, how to treat others, and how to make smart decisions.

What about Jesus?

In the Bible there are many characters with whom we will identify, but . . .

❓ Who is the true protagonist? To whom does all Scripture point?

Jesus. We will see that Jesus made the best decisions and that the entire Bible—even the entire Old Testament—speaks of him. In fact, that is why it is called "Old" because it was written before Jesus. Jesus decision to obey the Father and love us unconditionally brought salvation to the world, so make sure not to miss a single detail and you'll discover that the Bible, that collection of books, is the book of Jesus.

Challenge

While doing these studies, we will have time for devotionals during the week. It will be great if we could do them at home, setting aside a daily time (10 to 15 minutes) to read the proposed text, answer the questions, and take time to talk to God and answer in a personal way to the things the Bible tells us. This can transform us daily, and will prepare us for all good works!

Lesson 2 > GENESIS

The origin of everything

Genesis (from the Greek, "origin") could not have been a better title: it is the beginning of everything! The beginning of the universe, of humankind, of civilization, of the people of Israel, of sin, of the plan of salvation, etc.

The first book of the Bible introduces us fully to God's history, and is the first book of the Pentateuch (or Torah, in Hebrew), the first five books of the Bible that form a collection that was used by the people of Israel as a guide to make good decisions.

 Download complementary material for this section at www.e625.com/lessons.

Division and structure

In the beginning God created the heavens and the earth. **(Genesis 1: 1)**

The first eleven chapters of Genesis tell us about the history of the origins.

Chapters 1 and 2 are two versions of the same act: creation. They tell us about how God created everything that we see and do not see, and how he created human beings in his image. God made him free to love, and gave him only one commandment, on which he had to make a decision:

And the lord God commanded the man, "You are free to eat from any tree in the garden; but you must not eat from the tree of the knowledge of good and evil, for when you eat from it you will certainly die."
        (Genesis 2:16—17)

Every decision has its consequences.

What decision did Adam and Eve have to make, and what were its consequences?

But in chapter 3 comes temptation and disobedience. They took fruit from the tree from which they were commanded not to take it.

Why did they want to do precisely what they knew they shouldn't do?

Have you ever wanted to do what you are prohibited from doing? Why?

Lesson 2 > Genesis

Since then, human beings, who were in perfect harmony with God, with themselves, with each other, and with creation, broke down, because our decisions not only change our environment but also change us.

And that is our current situation: our relationship with God is broken, and so is our relationship with ourselves. We often do not do what we want, and it is difficult for us to decide what is right. Our relationship with our fellow men is also damaged. Often, our decisions hurt others. And lastly, creation also suffers from our free will.

How would you define free will, freedom?

After that moment, God draws near to transform the lives of men.

Up to the 11th chapter of Genesis we are told the consequences of this rupture:

- Cain and Abel in Chapter 4: Our decisions hurt or bless others.

- The story of Noah until chapter 10: God, despite human evil and its constant drift, saves Noah and his family, and they decide to trust in his word.

- The Tower of Babel in Chapter 11: everyone begins to speak different languages, and we no longer understand one another.

Here you can give an explanation (with a Bible in the hands of each of the adolescents). Stop at a specific story that you think is relevant to your current situation. If not, just mention it and move on.

From here we will be told the story of four characters who will be the main protagonists:

- Abraham: chapters 12 through 25
- Isaac: chapters 26 through 35 (although much of Jacob's life is told here)
- Jacob: chapters 27 through 36
- Joseph: chapters 37 through 50

The whole BIBLE in a year for HIGH SCHOOL

 Download the file at www.e625.com/lessons for an overview of Genesis, to be completed by the adolescents.

These characters will not be perfect:

- Abraham, the father of the faith, called by God to leave his land for another place. He obeyed God but sometimes his impatience made him make bad decisions, such as having a son with Hagar, his slave. In spite of everything, he was called God's friend, and he kept in mind what God taught him.

- Isaac, his son, will follow in his footsteps in doing many good things, but also some bad ones. In Genesis 26 we see that Isaac goes to a land called Gerar, and there he deceives people by saying that his wife is his sister!

 Why did he do it (verse 7)?

And you know what? His father Abraham had also done something similar.
Read Genesis 12:12–13. Isn't the similarity amazing?

Sometimes we make the same mistakes that our parents made. Many of us are children of believers, and our parents are often good examples. But we must write our own story with God, by making good decisions. If our parents made a bad decision, that is not an excuse for us to repeat their mistakes. Let's be wise and write our own story.

 Here, as the leader of the group, you could open your heart and tell an anecdote in which you decided to follow Jesus.

We must not live on borrowed faith; we must personally decide to follow Jesus.

 What does it mean to you to personally decide to follow Jesus?

- Jacob's story is like a TV soap opera. He was a liar, and often used lies to get his way, yet the lies always had consequences.

Do you remember any of the lies?

Jacob's story is well known. You don't need to stop too long here if you don't think it's necessary. Remember to be sensitive to the group.
- And finally there is the story of Joseph, a young man who constantly remained upright in his decisions, even though things were never easy for him.

What happened to Joseph, and what decision did he make?
Form groups of two or three teenagers, one for each text. Each one describes a moment in Joseph's life. Have them describe his problems and how he solved it.

Texts: (Download the template for each of the texts. Then each group can present its conclusions.)

Joseph was sold by his own brothers as a slave to Potiphar, an officer of Pharaoh, and from there things did not get any better:

> *Genesis 39: 1–6*
>
> *Genesis 39: 7–12*
>
> *Genesis 39: 19–23*
>
> *Genesis 40* (this text is longer, so give it to the fastest group, ha ha!)
>
> *Genesis 45: 1–14*

Thanks to these wise decisions of Joseph, Jacob (God changed his name to Israel) and his entire family went to live in Egypt and there they multiplied.

This will start the next book: Exodus.

What have you learned from the book of Genesis? Do you identify with any of the characters?

What about Jesus?

Joseph is very much like Jesus, who will be sold, betrayed, and will die as a slave. But, like Joseph, he will save his people. Jesus is the example of obedience, dedication, and perfect forgiveness to his brothers. Being the Lord, he does not punish but seeks to reconcile his brothers to himself.

Let's follow their example!

Decide

I decide to think wisely despite the circumstances, and to seek a personal relationship with Jesus, being responsible for my own life.

 To pray is a good decision. Take time to pray before dismissal.

 Some may want to pray for each other. You could have this dynamic in all the lessons, or in some of them. Remember to be sensitive to adolescent circumstances.

 Remember to download the daily readings, For Depth and Applications, from www.e625.com/lessons.

Lesson 3 > EXODUS AND LEVITICUS

A chosen people that God decided to liberate

Exodus

The history of the exodus is well known, and therefore I encourage you once again to give an overview of the subject and emphasize what you consider most important. Almost everyone knows the story of the exodus ("exit", in Greek), so here we give you the mental map of the book of Exodus.

Download complementary material for this section at www.e625.com/lessons. Internet resource: mental map to complete

The people of Israel were slaves in Egypt, and God decided (yes, God decides, and that is why we who are made in his image also decide things) to free his people from slavery. They had multiplied in those lands since Joseph had settled there with his entire family. Do you remember?

More than four hundred years had passed since then, and they were already a very numerous people, but they were enslaved. So God saved Moses from the waters as a baby, Moses lived in Pharaoh's house, and then made a bad decision: he took justice into his own hands (Exodus 2:11—15).

He fled to Midian and lived there for forty years, but God called him from a burning bush to free his people (Exodus 3:6—10).

God calls each of us for one purpose: to bless others. Moses made excuses.

What were those excuses (3:11; 4:1, 10, 13)?

Sometimes God calls us to make decisions, and we give him excuses. We do not want to have a personal relationship with him because that also implies responsibilities.

What excuses do we usually give to God?

I invite you to take all the time that you need for this. Give a personal example, and encourage participation. We are the masters at giving excuses!

Finally, Moses followed God's command, and then the ten plagues came. Does anyone remember them? Here is the list:

1 - *The waters turn to blood (Exodus 7:14—25)*
2 - *Frogs (Exodus 7:25; 8:1—15)*
3 - *Lice (Exodus 8:16—19)*
4 - *Flies (Exodus 8:20—32)*
5 - *Terrible pestilence on livestock (Exodus 9:1—7)*
6 - *Incurable boils and rashes (Exodus 9:8—12)*
7 - *Thunderstorm, hail, and fire (Exodus 9:13—35)*
8 - *Locusts (Exodus 10:1—20)*
9 - *Darkness for three days (Exodus 10:21—29)*
10 - *Death of the firstborn (Exodus 11:1—12; 29—51)*

Pharaoh finally let Israel go. They crossed the Red Sea and went to Sinai, and there they were given the Ten Commandments.

You don't need to read them, but use them as a resource.

You can schedule a day to see the movie "The Prince of Egypt"; it's a classic (and Mariah Carey and Whitney Houston sing!), so you don't have to explain the story too much.

Draw: How did you imagine God when you were a child? Then share it with others.

It can be a fun time, and also deep.

While waiting for Moses, the Israelites decided to build a golden calf, according to what they understood to be God.

Sometimes we want to build our lives based on our own criteria. We imagine God as we would like him to be, and we make decisions for ourselves regardless of what God is telling us for our good.

Look at the list of the ten commandments. They can be summarized as:

1) Loving God above all things
2) Loving your neighbor as yourself

Lesson 3 > Exodus and Leviticus

 Where would each of the Ten Commandments fit within these two categories?

 Use support material from the e625 website regarding the Ten Commandments, and place the commandments within the two categories.

Life is built on our decisions, and our decisions build our lives.

God left some guidelines to build the tabernacle, "the place of meeting with God," which was where the Israelites could communicate directly with him. He teaches us not only how to build the place in which we can meet with him but also how to approach it correctly. That's where the next book comes in.

Leviticus

The tribe of Levi was in charge of serving God and the rest of the twelve tribes, so that they could meet with God in the tabernacle. The whole book of Leviticus talks about this. Let's look at its structure.

 Download complementary material for this section at www.e625.com/lessons.

Let's learn from the example laid out in the book of Leviticus, and build our lives according to God's way of doing things, rather than our own.

 What would happen if we built a house without paying attention to the architect's plans? Would you trust that house? Would you go into that house?

 What would happen if we built our lives without paying attention to the plans of "The Architect"? Would you trust that life? Would you enter into that life?

The book of Leviticus is full of sacrifices. It sounds strange at first, but throughout these weeks we will see that decisions—all decisions—have consequences. Leviticus is an attempt to cover up the mistakes in people's decisions, but it will point to something else. Can you guess to what?

Leviticus, with its commandments and history, invites us to understand that God can free us from our slavery so that we can learn to live his way. He has decided to save us but he saved us for a purpose: to follow him, like the pillar of fire in the night, and also to love him and love our neighbor as ourselves, which is a summary of the Ten Commandments. Are we willing to make decisions according to his word, and not build our lives like Sinatra's song, "My Way"?

What about Jesus?

Yes, Jesus will be the final answer to the sacrifices. He will pay the consequences of our bad decisions, mistakes, and sins. He will lead us out of slavery, set us free, and guide us to follow his commandments. He is the Savior whom God sent to free his people. He is the rock on which we must build the house of our life so that it does not fall even when storms come. He will be the place where we'll meet with God, and his Word is the way of getting there.

What have you learned from the books of Exodus and Leviticus?

Decide

Let's remember this dynamic where adolescents can write on their notebook or tablet, or verbalize if they can about any decision they make based on what they have learned today.

To pray is a good decision. Take time to pray before dismissal.

Remember to download the daily readings, For Depth and Applications, from www.e625.com/lessons.

Lesson 4 > NUMBERS AND DEUTERONOMY

More than numbers

Numbers and Deuteronomy ("second law" in Greek) tell us the story of the forty years that the people of Israel spent in the desert because of their disobedience and (again) as a consequence of their decisions.

Moses may be the great legislator but he will also have to face complaints, criticism, cowardice, rebellion, and the many things that take place when your mission is to lead a group.

Look at the wrong turn that they made!

Download complementary material for this section at www.e625.com/lessons.

Life is a journey to get somewhere, and sometimes we feel that this journey takes us through a desert. The people of Israel went through it for real. During that journey they lived through many challenges, and God spoke to them in many ways. Also, they had to make many important decisions during their journey.

Remember to share the mental map of Numbers and Deuteronomy so that they can complete it during the session.

Numbers

Permanence at Sinai (1:1—10:10)
After taking a census to determine who the people were (that's why the book is called "Numbers"), Moses shared a series of laws and reminders, including the celebration of Passover in Numbers 9.

Do you remember what happened in Egypt during the last plague?

During the Passover meal, God rescued and saved the firstborn through the sacrifice of one lamb per family.

Does that mean anything to us today?

Remember to connect these books—especially those that are particularly dense—to Jesus. We want them to see the importance of studying the Bible, even the book of Numbers! Jesus will be the sacrifice, our Passover. He will free us.

The cloud by day and the pillar of fire by night settled over the tabernacle when it was erected, and when the cloud moved the Israelites moved, and when it did not move they did not move (Numbers 9:21).

Life in the desert was about deciding whether to trust the cloud (God's presence) or to take their chances going through the desert on their own.

What can be the dangers of going through the desert on our own?

To be a Christian means to follow Jesus and his presence, and trust that he is going to lead us in his ways. Do we trust him more than we trust ourselves?

The long march to Moab (10:11—21:35)

God always provides for us: in the desert he sent the manna, and in Numbers 11 he even sent quail.

But not everything is rosy: Moses own brothers will murmur about the decisions he makes.

What are murmurs? Why are they dangerous?

Now we come to a very sad and important point in the story. Numbers 13 tells us that twelve explorers were sent to the promised land to report on what they saw there. Among them were two young men, Joshua and Caleb. Other than those two, all of them saw the taking of the promised land as impossible. Even though God had promised them the land, the people rebelled, and they did not have the courage to say yes to God. They did not enter the promised land. Not to make a decision is already a decision.

The consequence of deciding not to enter it was that none of those who were part of God's people at that time (other than Joshua and Caleb) ever entered the promised land. They spent forty years in the desert because of their decision!

Lesson 4 > Numbers and Deuteronomy

 What decisions do we postpone? For example: studying at the last minute for an exam, telling the truth to someone at some point, admitting a mistake.

Often to postpone a decision until later is a bad decision.

Numbers teaches us the consequences of not following God's path and preferring to stay as we are (we will also see the rebellion of Korah in Numbers 16).

 What do you understand as rebellion? What was the consequence of that particular rebellion? (Numbers 16: 31—32)

Often, our decision to become rebellious brings judgment to our life. We may not realize it at the time, but when we decide to break with the people who can take care of us and guide us, it destroys us. Do you know of any case or example of rebellion?

On the plains of Moab (22:1—36:13)

On the plains of Moab a curious character appears: Balaam, who out of self-interest was going to curse Israel on behalf of King Balak. But God stopped him, and here comes the famous story of the talking donkey! All because Balaam did not want to listen to God.

Sometimes God speaks to us through other people (and this does not mean that they are donkeys.), But often we are so blind, wanting to make decisions based on self-interest, that God puts people at our side to warn us.

 Who do you think are the people God has put around you to help you make good decisions?

After many turns, some tribes had already settled in the place where they would live, and that's when the last book of the Pentateuch begins, a kind of last will from Moses, as ordained by God.

Deuteronomy

Here, Moses is constantly exhorting us to obedience (he also tells us about some battles, but the central point is the invitation to obedience, and the dangers and risks of disobedience). He also invites us to follow the commandments (and he repeated them in Deuteronomy 5).

It is good to remember that everything that Moses (and God) says is for the good of his people and not on a whim, which is why in this book we find masterful phrases that Jesus himself will recover.

Does anyone know which is the first of all commandments?

It can be found in Deuteronomy 6:4—5. How important is this book!

And check also Deuteronomy 10:12—13.

What do you think this means?

God is not interested in helping us only in one area of our life. He wants to take care of us and guide us in everything.

Deuteronomy talks about many situations: what to do with poverty, how to deal with practices that are not right for us, laws about animals, about war, about the economy, about sexual behavior, etc.

We will often have to make decisions in all these areas, and that is why God wants to give us his wisdom.

At the end of the book, Moses names his successor: Joshua, that young man who dared to enter the promised land, and who was not so young now but still had the same courage.

So in chapter 32 Moses sings a very long song, longer than a rap (was Moses a singer?), because he was grateful for God's faithfulness.

That is why he praises God, being able to contemplate the land of Canaan, and blessing each tribe that he led there, until in chapter 34 his days come to an end. And what an end!

> *Since then, no prophet has risen in Israel like Moses, whom the Lord knew face to face, who did all those signs and wonders the Lord sent him to do in Egypt—to Pharaoh and to all his officials and to his whole land. For no one has ever shown the mighty power or performed the awesome deeds that Moses did in the sight of all Israel.*

He was not perfect, but he learned to be guided by God to make decisions. I hope that all of us will want to follow his example.

Lesson 4 > Numbers and Deuteronomy

What about Jesus?

Many of the things we see in Numbers and Deuteronomy point to Jesus. For example, the Passover—which rescued Israel by grace—and the cloud by day and the pillar of fire by night—which we must follow in the desert. And Jesus will remind us of the importance of the most important commandment, from Deuteronomy 6:4—5.

Decide

I decide to follow God and read the Bible not to postpone the important decisions in my life, and to always continue to go wherever he leads me.

What has caught your attention the most in this week's lesson?

To pray is a good decision. Take time to pray before dismissal.

Remember to download the daily readings, For Depth and Applications, from www.e625.com/lessons.

Lesson 5 > JOSHUA

We must also have initiative!

A new stage begins. Joshua, the new leader, must face a new way of doing things. The Israelites are no longer in the desert; they are at the gates of the promised land, and this will demand another style of leadership, another side of the coin, in order to make decisions.

Division and structure

Download complementary material for this section at www.e625.com/lessons.

Look at the mental map.

The first thing we find are some words of encouragement that many already know, and that we must remember:

> Keep this Book of the Law always on your lips; meditate on it day and night, so that you may be careful to do everything written in it. Then you will be prosperous and successful. Have I not commanded you? Be strong and courageous. Do not be afraid; do not be discouraged, for the Lord your God will be with you wherever you go. (Joshua 1:8—9)

First, God invites us not to deviate from the Book of the Law, that is, not to deviate from the way of life that he indicates for us (for Joshua it was the Pentateuch; for us today it is the whole Word of God). And not just to read it, but to meditate on it.

What are the differences between reading and meditating? Why is it important to meditate?

But it's not juts meditate on it but also to obey it. The Bible was not written only to be studied but, as we have seen previously, to be obeyed. Verse 9 is great; it encourages us to be strong and brave. Many times, cowardice gives us away and plays tricks on us. Facing life's challenges will require a value system that can only be achieved within the security of his Word. And finally, there is a promise: "The Lord your God will be with you wherever you go."

This is a very strong statement! Earlier, Moses followed the cloud, but now God himself says that he will be with us: not only us with Him, but he with us! If we keep his Word and obey it and take the initiative with courage, He will be with us. God had opened the Red Sea and now they had to cross the Jordan River, but the waters would not open up until the sole of the priests' feet touched the water (Joshua 3:13).

Many of us would like to see it happen the other way around, right? Let the water separate first and then we can walk. But in life we should always walk by faith, making decisions in the midst of uncertainty, trusting God. This is the great challenge.

And that's how Joshua crossed the Jordan River.

In what situations should we wet the soles of our feet before the waters separate (for example: what to study, what friends to choose, etc.)?

If we have the right principles, we will be able to make the right decisions, and the right principles are in God's Word.

God inspired Joshua to fight his battles. Everyone remembers Jericho, the seven times going around the city, the shouts, the spies (chapters 2 and 6), etc., but there were other battles such as that of Ai (chapter 8), against the Amorites (chapter 10), that of Jabin (chapter 11) , etc.

One can get the mistaken impression that it was quick, an easy conquest, but it wasn't easy at all. There were plenty of problems and it took a long time.

Following Jesus is not going to be an easy path: sometimes it will cost us, and we will make mistakes, but we must be persistent. Following Jesus will not take away our problems, because that's not his promise. His promise is that he will be with us. Always. He will accompany us.

It is amazing that the Lord of heaven and earth decides to accompany us in our decisions. That gives us hope to keep going.

Up until chapter 22, Joshua will be devoted to organizing the territory, instituting the cities of refuge and those for the Levites. Not everything can be moving forward, fighting battles, winning them, etc; you also have to organize. If we do not have an organized life, it is very difficult to keep going.

This is also something that we have to decide! If we simply move forward without organizing our lives, everything will end up being chaos. In order to continue making good decisions, it is important to organize and distribute our strengths and our time well.

? **How do we organize our days? And our week? Or, are we rather disorganized?**

Many of us waste a lot of time because we are not well organized.

Organization File

Download complementary material for this section at www.e625.com/lessons.

? **When you look at your schedule, what comes to mind? In which areas do you think you need to improve in order to be more effective?**

? **What are the advantages of being better organized?**

At the end of the book, Joshua exhorts the people to continue striving to do all that is written in the Book of the Law (23:6), and challenges them to make a choice between the gods of others and God, between living under other principles, or those of his Word.

Read Joshua 24:14–15.

? **Why should the people listen to Joshua (vv. 16–18)? God was the one who delivered them; He is the true God, the only one who saved them.**

Let's remember that we follow Jesus because he saved us first. We do not serve him to earn his favor, but because we already have it.

What about Jesus?

God appeared to Moses in a burning bush. The commander of the Lord's army appeared to Joshua (Joshua 5:14). Who do you think he is? He said, "Take off your shoes," just like God told Moses.

Although Joshua took charge, he was very clear that God was really in charge, and he knew who the Lord was.

Decide

I decide to be hard-working and courageous, to take charge of my life based on the principles of the Word of God, keeping a real relationship alive to be able to follow Jesus.

Lesson 5 > Joshua

 What have you learned this week?

 To pray is a good decision. Take time to pray before dismissal.

 Remember to download the daily readings, For Depth and Applications, from www.e625.com/lessons.

Lesson 6 > JUDGES

The book of imperfect heroes

When the twelve tribes settled in the promised land they did not have a king. Each tribe functioned autonomously and they were united by the ark, the service of the tribe of Levi, and the united front they sometimes formed to fight battles.

God raised up judges (from the Hebrew *shofetim*), although in reality we should not imagine that they were judges like those we have today. The best translation would be "heroes." These heroes ruled temporarily. They were people chosen by God to lead the people of Israel and get them out of trouble.

The narrative of the book of Judges is almost always the same.

1. *The people are faithful to God, usually under a good judge (starting with Joshua).*

2. *When the judge dies, the people become unfaithful, forget about God, and make decisions on their own.*

3. *Then God, who respects our decisions, hands them over to their enemies.*

4. *The people then repent and cry out to God, and God raises up another judge to save them.*

Download complementary material for this section at www.e625.com/lessons.

In the circle that you've downloaded you can see this dynamic of Judges.

Does this dynamic remind you of anything? Does our life look like this? Why do you think this happens to us?

Will we always live like this?

Lesson 6 > Judges

Division and structure

Here is the mental map of Judges with its protagonists:

- Introduction to the period of the judges (1:1 to 3:6)
- Israel's judges (3:7–16)
- From Othniel to Shamgar
- Deborah
- Gideon and Abimelech
- Tola and Jair
- Jephthah
- From Ibzan to Abdon
- Samson
- The finish (17–21)

Download the incomplete map from www.e625.com/lessons for the adolescents to work on.

Not all the judges are given the same attention, because we all remember Gideon, who with three hundred men was able to fight against the Midianites, but hardly anybody knows Tola.

This week it would be great to invite each young person to get to know one of the judges through the Scriptures.

The last of the judges who appear in the book is Samson.

We all remember him: his birth was announced by an angel. (Interestingly, throughout the Old Testament no one else was announced by an angel, and in the New Testament only John the Baptist and Jesus had this honor!)

Samson was born a Nazirite, set apart for God. The Nazirite oath was a vow to be dedicated exclusively to Jehovah.

We all know that when the Spirit of Jehovah came upon Samson, he had superhuman strength. He was quite a hero, almost a superhero, with superpowers and everything! The expectations placed on him were very high. But we all know how it ended. Why? Because of the decisions that he made.

As we begin his story in Judges 14:1 we see that "Samson went down . . .", and this is the summary of his life: he took a downward path because of his bad decisions.

There were two dangers that affected his life, and we are going to study them in this lesson, as they can also be dangers for us. Let's read about the first one.

> When he returned, he said to his father and mother, "I have seen a Philistine woman in Timnah; now get her for me as my wife."
> His father and mother replied,
> "Isn't there an acceptable woman among your relatives or among all our people? Must you go to the uncircumcised Philistines to get a wife?"
> But Samson said to his father, "Get her for me. She's the right one for me."
> (Judges 14:2–3)

This last sentence is the key. To fall in love is not the problem, the problem is why Samson does it. And the reason is . . . because he wants to. As simple as that. Since that's how he feels, it must be true; if his heart tells him to do it, it must be the right thing to do.

It reminds me of many items of clothing teenagers now wear: "Follow your heart," or as a Disney prince would say to a Disney princess: "Do whatever your heart tells you to do." No! That's a serious mistake.

However, how many times do we let ourselves be led by what our heart dictates?

Today this philosophy is in vogue: "If you feel like it, do it. It's the truth." But this can have terrible consequences for us. How often does our heart tell us one thing one day, and another thing the next day? Elsewhere in the Bible we will see that our hearts are deceitful and that we cannot trust them.

> The heart is deceitful above all things,
> and beyond cure.
> Who can understand it?
>
> (Jeremiah 17:9)

When do you think our hearts can deceive us? How does our heart affect our decision-making?

Do you know any stories of people who made decisions based on "what their heart likes"?

The second danger comes from the outside.

Lesson 6 > Judges

In Judges 14, after starting a relationship with that woman, Samson throws a party. Having a party is not a bad thing, the problem is in why we do it. We read in verse 10:

> Now his father went down to see the woman. And there Samson held a feast, as was customary for young men.

Why did he do it? Out of habit, peer pressure, because others do it.
It is well known that virtually all mothers in the world, when their children do something because their friends do it, will ask:

"Son, if your friends jumped off a bridge, would you do it too?"

This is how our mothers are, but even if it is difficult for us to admit it,
they are right.

Many times we make decisions not because it's what we want, but because we let ourselves be carried by the current. We believe that our ideas, thoughts, decisions, etc., are our own, but 95% of them are only retweets from people who have passed them on to us, from Facebook stories, from fashion, from musical styles, from what we are told is the meaning of life. . . . We believe that we are independent, but many times we only follow the current fashion, and then we think that we are unique.

What is a retweet? In which areas of our lives do we allow ourselves to follow what others do?

These two dangers slowly led Samson to his ruin, and he almost didn't even realize it, after the story of Delilah that almost everyone knows.

Is it necessary to tell that story? If so, do it quickly.

Samson ended up caught by the Philistines, blind, tied to a mill in jail, going around in circles.

> Then the Philistines seized him, gouged out his eyes and took him down to Gaza. Binding him with bronze shackles, they set him to grinding grain in the prison. But the hair on his head began to grow again after it had been shaved. (Judges 16:21–22)

And that's the way many of our friends find themselves, right? Or maybe even ourselves.

- *Blind: without seeing what is in front of us, without knowing what to do.*

- *Tied up: to things that we cannot stop doing.*

- *Going around in circles: without any clear direction for our lives.*

If the story had ended here, it would be one of the saddest stories in the Bible, but it didn't. Scripture says that his hair began to grow again.

What do you think it means that Samson's hair began to grow? Why does the Bible mention it? It is important?

The idea is that Samson was able to reflect on his situation, and he was able to reconsider. Samson's hair was not "magic" but it was the last symbol left of his Nazirite oath.

How did the story end (Judges 16:23–31, especially verse 30)?

Samson sacrificed himself to fulfill his mission.

What do you think were his biggest mistakes?

How do you think we can avoid those mistakes in our own decisions?

What about Jesus?

Jesus will be our ultimate hero. He will be the last judge. He sacrificed himself for us. His birth was announced by an angel, and he came to save his people. His super—power is to give life, and during his time on earth he gave a lot of life to people, but through his death he gave eternal life. May Jesus be our hero! And he is also a judge who, far from judging, will himself be judged for our guilt.

Listen on YouTube to "Heroe", by Alex Sampedro.

Decide

I choose to be guided by the Word of God and not by what my heart or social pressure dictates. To pray is a good decision. Take time to pray before dismissal.

Remember to download the daily readings, For Depth and Applications, from www.e625.com/lessons.

Lesson 7 > 1 AND 2 SAMUEL

The time of the judges ends, the era of the kings begins

The time of the judges will come to an end, and the last judge will rise: Samuel, a prophet who will judge the people but who at their request will give them a king, which is what they asked for.

This king will be Saul. But Saul will end up despising God, and Samuel, inspired by God, will anoint a new king, David. Yes, the famous King David.

Download complementary material for this section at www.e625.com/lessons.

What do you remember about King David?

Despite his ups and downs, his mistakes and his sins, David was a man after God's own heart.

These three characters will occupy the leading role in this book of Samuel distributed in two volumes. We will learn a lot from them: how they were brave and guided by God, and also how they walked away and how they returned, how they made mistakes and corrected their mistakes.
We can easily identify with them.

Division and structure

Download the book's structure from www.e625.com/lessons.

Mental map.

1 Samuel
Samuel's childhood; prophet and judge (1–7)
Hannah was unable to have children, but God granted Samuel to her, and she dedicated him to Jehovah. Samuel was to be raised by Eli, God's priest, in Silo, where the ark of the covenant was at that time.

What is the Ark of the Covenant?

In 1 Samuel 3:3–4 we read:

> ...and Samuel was lying down in the house of the Lord, where the ark of God was.
>
> Then the Lord called Samuel.
>
> Samuel answered, "Here I am."

At first Samuel thought that Eli was the one who had called him, and it was Eli himself who explained that it was actually God. Samuel learned to listen to the voice of God, to distinguish it from other voices, and to follow it.

Eli's sons were not very good followers of their father, and finally Samuel was made a judge of Israel and a prophet (1 Samuel 7).

But...

Institution of the monarchy (8–12)

Israel asked for a king. They no longer wanted judges. Do you know why the Israelites didn't have a king? Because God was their king!

Why did the Israelites want a king (1 Samuel 1:19)?

The chosen one was Saul. Apparently he had everything needed to be the king of Israel. He was anointed by Samuel and defeated the Ammonites, a people who were oppressing the Israelites.

Saul's reign (13–15)

But all that glitters is not gold. Saul disobeyed God since he wanted to do things his way, and Samuel had to say to Saul:

> *Does the Lord delight in burnt offerings and sacrifices as much as in obeying the Lord?*
> *To obey is better than sacrifice, and to heed is better than the fat of rams.*
> *For rebellion is like the sin of divination, and arrogance like the evil of idolatry.*
> *Because you have rejected the word of the Lord, he has rejected you as king.*
> (1 Samuel 15:22–23)

Lesson 7 > 1 and 2 Samuel

 What pleases the Lord the most? Why?

David is anointed King (16–31)
Once Saul is rejected, Samuel, led by God, anoints David, the youngest in the house of Jesse.

Samuel thought the new king was going to be one of David's older brothers.

> But the Lord said to Samuel, "Do not consider his appearance or his height, for I have rejected him. The Lord does not look at the things people look at. People look at the outward appearance, but the Lord looks at the heart." (1 Samuel 16:7)

 What differences are there between looking at appearances and looking at people's hearts?

 To make good decisions, why should we focus on the heart and not on appearances? David did many great things, he killed the giant Goliath and Saul was envious of him. David had to flee and, although he was the Lord's anoin—ted, he went through a process in which he learned that what was important was not the position he occupied but the people he served. He was always aware of others.

On some occasions David had the opportunity to harm Saul, and he chose not to, because he respected him. God tested David for a time before making him king.

 **Why do you think this is important? What process did Saul go through to become king?**

 This is a good place to point out the importance of processes, and of having patience in our lives. Adolescents are going through a time in their lives in which they may know what they want, but they must focus on training and preparation. They must learn how to live with the frustration of not being able to do it yet, while also learning to take advantage of the service opportunities that are offered to them to take care of others, even though the situation is not ideal.

2 SAMUEL
David's reign begins (1–8)
Saul dies in a complicated situation, and David is crowned king of Judah. Thus begins the second book of Samuel.

David's reign (9–20)

Despite being the most famous king of Israel, David went through many dark moments during his reign. One of his best-known stumbles was the one he committed with Bathsheba, and in chapter 11 we read the story.

Focus on the story as you see fit, depending on the characteristics of your group of teens.

We are taught that David, at a time when kings went to war, chose to stay in the palace, which was the beginning of his problem. If we do not do what we should be doing, temptations may show up, out of boredom!

When you have nothing to do, what are things that you want to do that you know are not right?

If you think this is a very direct question, a good tool is to ask the question in the third person:

For example, when a teenager has nothing to do, what things do you think he is tempted to do?

As always, decisions have consequences, and although God's mercy always helps us and takes care of us, mistakes can haunt us, as we saw in the case of David.

One of David's sons, Absalom, rebelled against him, and he spent many of his last years paying the price for not having taken care of his family as well as he had taken care of his kingdom.

David finally emerged victorious, and was able to return to the city of Jerusalem.

Psalm 18 and the census (21–24)

At the end of the book there is a psalm, and one last mistake made by David: he conducted a military census.

It was a mistake because he trusted in his abilities as a human, in his army, and in his people instead of trusting in God's help, which had always been decisive in his life.

The consequence was that death came, and it was stopped by God's mercy outside Jerusalem, in the field of a man named Araunah.
David bought that field and built an altar there. That was the place where Solomon would later build the temple.

Lesson 7 > 1 and 2 Samuel

Important questions, important decisions

In what areas have you identified with David's life? What do we learn from his successes and failures?

Why does the Bible say that David was a man "after God's own heart"?

What about Jesus?

The people rejected God as their king, because they wanted a man as their king. But instead, Jesus, God incarnate, will be the king we really need. One of the titles that we will use to talk about Jesus is "son of David." Only Jesus will be the infallible king who can bring to his people the justice, peace, and joy that they need.

Decide

I decide not to waste my time during my youth, to take advantage of it to prepare myself and to have the patience to build who I am going to be, knowing the danger that "staying in the palace when the kings go to war" entails. Lord, help me not to get taken away by the current, but to become a man "after your heart."

To pray is a good decision. Take time to pray before dismissal.

Remember to download the daily readings, For Depth and Applications, from www.e625.com/lessons.

Lesson 8 > 1 AND 2 KINGS

Who is the king?

Solomon succeeded David and built the temple, the spiritual center of the nation. He asked God for wisdom to rule. His forty-year reign was the most prosperous for the people of Israel, but even though he was the wisest man on earth, he made a serious mistake: he allowed himself to be guided by his own heart.

He had. . . a thousand women! And all at the same time! And at the end of his days, he fell into idolatry. After his reign there was some fighting, the kingdom was divided: Judah to the south and Israel to the north. Follies result in division.

After that, kings of the north and south succeeded each other, and for better or worse all were very human. I love the books of Kings because they get real, they talk about kings and the hits and misses that they had. In this lesson we will study what some did, and the consequences that their actions brought.

In the midst of these stories, two prophets appeared: Elijah in the first book and Elisha, his successor, in the second. Both these characters starred in many of the stories, during what were dark times for the nation. The Assyrians were their most feared and cruel enemies, and they ended up conquering God's people due to the Israelites' idolatry.

At the end of the second book we will watch with amazement how Jerusalem falls and how God's people are deported to Babylon, but this will not be the end for them.

Review the structure
Download complementary material for this section at www.e625.com/lessons.

 *Breaking down a king:*

> Create work teams of two to four adolescents (depending on the size of the group), and choose the story of a king from those suggested below. (No more than four or five teams.) Have them read the text and complete the sheet from the website, and then present it to everyone else.
>
> **Questions:** *Who is the king? What do we know about his family? What good decisions did he make? What bad decisions did he make? What were the consequences? What kind of relationship did he have with God?*

Lesson 8 > 1 and 2 Kings

Process: *read the text; group discussion to complete the presentation; present it to all; conclusions.*

Kings:

- Asa (1 Kings 15:9–23)
- Ahab (1 Kings 16:29–33)
- Jehoshaphat (1 Kings 22:41–50)
- Hezekiah (2 Kings 18:1–8)
- Manasseh (2 Kings 21:1–18)
- Josiah (2 Kings 22:1–10, 23:1–8)

What has caught your attention about this dynamic? What do we learn from it?

Elijah and Elisha were the prophets who spoke on behalf of God with some of these kings that we've learned about. Many of the kings did not listen to the prophets, but these prophets, despite the problems they faced, remained faithful to their calling. Through miracles and signs they tried to warn the kings of the consequences of their bad actions. God did not give up on saving his people.

What were the differences between some kings and others? Can we also fall into some kind of idolatry and disregard God? How?

What about Jesus?

After so many examples of failure and imperfection, and the deportation to Babylon, it became increasingly clear that there was a need for a Savior, a king, a priest, a prophet, a son of David, to restore his people. Jesus was the answer to all our mistakes and failures, being the King of Kings.

Decide

I decide not to fall into idolatry or allow other things to be in the holy place that belongs only to God, to follow again the guidance of his Word, and let him rule my life.

 To pray is a good decision. Take time to pray before dismissal.

 Remember to download the daily readings, For Depth and Applications, from www.e625.com/lessons.

Lesson 9 > JOB

A painful dialogue

In this session it is important that they bring their physical Bible, since they are going to handle it a lot in order to be able to perform the different dynamics. Remind them through their social network group, WhatsApp, or another app.

Do bad things happen to bad people and good things happen to good people? If you behave well, will everything go well for you?

Why is there suffering in the world? Why does God allow it? Whose fault is it that there is suffering?

Video of an impressionist painting. You only see a portion, a stain. Something that seems dirty. Toward the end of the session the image is enlarged and the beauty of the full painting is seen. This will help us explain that moments of pain cannot be understood on their own. That there is a larger framework that we are not able to understand, but from God's perspective he is painting a beautiful picture.

Download at www.e625.com/lessons the complementary material for this section.

These are the questions that this book raises, and they are some of the most important questions that we face. The story of Job is presented to us as if it were a play; he was a man from the Orient, just and upright. We see in the first act that Satan, the accuser, stands before God and accuses Job of being just only because everything is going well for him. He argues that if Job's blessings were taken away, he would deny God. Job is put to the test and loses practically everything: his fortune, his family (except his wife), his health, his property.

Then three of his friends arrive. Bildad, Zophar, and Eliphaz, take turns arguing with Job in order to convince him that all that is happening to him is because he has done something evil. The conversation gets heated, with interruptions, arguments, attacks, and defenses. Suddenly a young man appears, Elihu, who seems more sensible than the other friends, and then, surprisingly, God himself joins the conversation to explain himself. In the end, Job recognizes God's sovereignty in spite of his circumstances, and God restores his situation, blessing him with much more than what he previously had.

Lesson 9 > Job

Look at the structure of this story and the pace of conversation, arguments, and position.

Introduction (1:1–5)
We are introduced to the protagonist, Job, and his attitudes.

What was Job like?

Job's first and second trials. Appearance of the three friends (1:6–2:13)
The narrative takes us into God's presence, where the action takes place. God praises Job and Satan accuses him of being righteous out of personal interest. Satan makes Job suffer in various ways, and then returns to the presence of God. Job remains firm, and Satan returns to Job to touch his health, virtually the only thing he has left.

This is how it happened:

> *So Satan went out from the presence of the Lord and afflicted Job with painful sores from the soles of his feet to the crown of his head. Then Job took a piece of broken pottery and scraped himself with it as he sat among the ashes.*
>
> *His wife said to him, "Are you still maintaining your integrity? Curse God and die!"*
>
> *He replied, "You are talking like a foolish woman. Shall we accept good from God, and not trouble?"*
>
> *In all this, Job did not sin in what he said. (Job 2:7–10)*

If you were Job's friend, what would you have said to him at that moment?

His three friends arrived and stayed by his side in silence for seven full days, without saying anything. Then. . .

Job's first speech (3)

Job bemoans his situation, and is sincere about his feelings and questions:

> "Why is light given to those in misery, and life to the bitter of soul, to those who long for death that does not come [...].?" (Job 3:20)

Why do you think it is important to be honest before God?

Then there is a dialogue between Job and his friends, in which they basically try to explain his situation, alluding to the fact that he may have done something evil. Job defends his position, and tries to give an explanation for what is happening.

Divide the group into four teams. Each team chooses one of Job's friends, and one of their speeches. They read it and find out what the arguments and accusations against Job are. What does Job's friend believe? Why does he think this is happening to Job? They should support their answer by mentioning the verses. (In the case of Elihu, choose one chapter.)

Here's all the discussion, which is the bulk of the book. This is how it happens:

Print the structure

- Eliphaz's first speech (4–5)
- Job's second speech (6–7)
- Bildad's first speech (8)
- Job's third speech (9–10)
- Zophar's first speech (11)
- Job's fourth speech (12–14)
- Eliphaz's second speech (15)
- Job's fifth speech (16–17)
- Bildad's second speech (18)
- Job's sixth speech (19)
- Zophar's second speech (20)
- Job's seventh speech (21)
- Eliphaz's third speech (22)
- Job's eighth speech (23:1–24:17)
- Zophar's interruption (24:18—25)
- Bildad's third speech (25)
- Job's interruption (26:1–4)
- Bildad continues (26:5–14)
- Job's ninth speech (27:1–12)

Lesson 9 > Job

- Zophar's third speech (27:13–23)
- In praise of Wisdom (28)
- Job's soliloquy (29–31)
- Elihu's intervention–four speeches (32–37)

Download complementary material for this section at www.e625.com/lessons.

What is empathy?

In this lesson, take the opportunity to work on the concept of not judging others over their situation, of learning to put yourself in the place of the other, and of not being like Job's friends. It is possible that Job was not right about everything, but the attitude of his friends shows a lack of sensitivity and fairness when dealing with him

When a friend or a relative is having a hard time, how do we react? How should we react?

After the involvement of all of Job's friends, God himself intervenes.

God's response (38–41)
God himself answers Job.

> "Where were you when I laid the earth's foundation?
> Tell me, if you understand." (Job 38:4)

God's answer is surprising: he does not address Job's suffering, but affirms his wisdom, greatness, faithfulness, and other attributes that he possesses. God gives a broader framework of the situation by making us see that we do not have the capacity to understand everything.

Very often things happen in our life that we do not fully understand, but God's eternal perspective gives us hope.

The impressionist painting that at first we saw only as a stain now becomes a work of art.

Job's Answer (42:1–6)

> *My ears had heard of you but now my eyes have seen you. (Job 42:5.)*

Epilogue (42:7–16)
The story ends well. God restores Job's life in many ways: his family, his wealth, and his social life. Job prays for his friends, he has new daughters and sons, and above all he recognizes God.

What has caught your attention the most in Job's story?

What about Jesus?
Read Job 33:23–28.

Here you can allude to our need for a savior, a redeemer, someone who pays our debts, who shows us God's mercy, to make us like children. It is pure Gospel.
Job is poetry, a literary masterpiece that points to God who will lose everything while being just, who will save and intercede for his "friends" (and enemies) who were accusing him, and who in the end will restore all things.

Decide

I decide to put my life in God's hands and trust him in the midst of adversity and doubts. I know that there are things that are difficult to understand, but I want to know God better and to see him in the midst of my life's circumstances.

To learn more: *The Problem of Pain* (C. S. Lewis)

To pray is a good decision. Take time to pray before dismissal.

Remember to download the daily readings, For Depth and Applications, from www.e625.com/lessons.

Lesson 10 > PSALMS

Poetry and creativity

The book of Psalms (*Tehillim*, in Hebrew) is full of creativity. Any composer would want his songs to continue to be sung thousands of years after he wrote them, and those who composed the psalms achieved this. In addition, it is a very important book, and it's the book quoted the most by Jesus in the Gospels.

The music and sound have not come down to us, although there are some indications in the Bible about how to sing them, based on popular melodies from those times.

What has survived has been the poetry, the lyrics, and the message, which continue to inspire millions of people to have a real living relationship with God.

Download at www.e625.com/lessons the complementary material for this section.

Do you remember any song or song lyrics that come from a psalm?

Division and structure

Psalms is divided into five books. Each of them ends with a doxology, a hymn of praise to God.

Here is the structure of the book of Psalms:

- Book 1: chapters 1 through 41
- Book 2: chapters 42 through 72
- Book 3: chapters 73 through 89
- Book 4: chapters 90 through 106
- Book 5: chapters 107 through 150

What do you believe are the themes covered in the book of Psalms?

One of the objectives is for us to see the richness of the Psalms, and how they cannot be reduced just to praising God, but in addition speak to many of the issues that affect us as human beings.

Watch on YouTube the video of Bono's meeting with Eugene Peterson.
You can play the whole video (about twenty minutes) or part of it, depending on the objectives of your session and on the group you are leading.

What do you think of the video? What has caught your attention the most?

Why do you think it is important to study the Psalms today?

Do you see any difference between the songs we sing now in our congregations and the psalms? What is the difference?

Types of psalms:

There are many types of psalms, not only psalms of worship, like 103. There are also psalms of thanksgiving (18), psalms of prayer (90), psalms of repentance (51), historical psalms (108), psalms that emphasize Jehovah's reign (24), confidence psalms (130), messianic psalms (2), wisdom psalms (119), and other more complex ones, such as psalms of imprecation or curse (109), reflecting the real feelings of the psalmists at that moment.

 You can have the students look them up, read them, and find the different themes, the richness, and the variety of the psalms.

 **Do you think that today we are as sincere in our communication with God as the psalmist were? Why?**

The creativity in the book of Psalms is amazing. For the Hebrews, the rhyme was in the ideas, and that's why they used many parallelisms or puns. They understood that creativity and beauty were also a gift from God, and they made poetry to reflect the characteristics of their God.

As you have seen, the psalmists were extremely sincere: they stayed far away from religiousness and expressed their thoughts, with fear of God but without hypocrisy.

 **How sincere do you think our relationship with God is today? What can we do to live our relationship with God like the psalmists did?**

What about Jesus?

As we've already mentioned, the book of Psalms is the one most quoted by Jesus. Many psalms speak of Jesus and have their fulfillment in him, and many can only be understood if they are placed on his lips, and in the light of his life. It is because of Jesus that we can sing, praise, and express ourselves with confidence before God, and that is why the book of Psalms is the book of songs about Jesus.

Decide

I decide to live the truth of the book of Psalms, confidently expressing myself before God with sincerity and reverence. I decide to creatively reflect our creator God, and to create art that lives up to the Gospel message that we represent.

 To pray is a good decision. Take time to pray before dismissal.

 Remember to download the daily readings, For Depth and Applications, from www.e625.com/lessons.

Lesson 11 > PROVERBS

Wisdom in 140 characters (more or less)

Practical tips. For now, for me. Faith in God is not a theoretical idea that does not affect our daily life and our decisions. Quite the opposite, since it is eminently practical. The Bible proposes a way of living, not just a series of dogmas.

Proverbs is that amazing book that can help you make the best decisions in practically all areas of life: sexuality, finances, interpersonal and business relationships, as well as work, rest, study, family, etc. It covers a multitude of topics and in a viral way, ahead of all those viral phrases that spread throughout the internet like wildfire.

Proverbs provides short phrases, easy-to-remember couplets, and wisdom "tweets" that help us in practical terms to "become wise."

Download at www.e625.com/lessons the complementary material for this section.

What do you think wisdom is?

Wisdom is not about having a lot of information; rather, it is about learning how to live, and this is what Proverbs proposes: the art of living, the beginning of wisdom in order to make better decisions.

What is the opposite of wisdom? Why is it important to be wise in life?

Is there a proverb that you remember? Which one? Why?

Consider sharing a verse from Proverbs that has helped you personally, and invite the teens to do the same.

Division and structure

The book of Proverbs is divided into several collections of proverbs, some very long and others rather short. Its structure is very simple:

- Introduction (1:1–7)
- First collection: Poems (1:8–9:18)
- Second collection: Proverbs of Solomon (10:1–22:16)
- Third collection: The words of the wise (22:17–24:22)

- Fourth collection: Sayings of the wise (24:23–34)
- Fifth collection: Proverbs of Solomon (25:1–29:27)
- Sixth collection: The words of Agur (30:1–33)
- Seventh collection: The words of King Lemuel (31:1–9)
- Appendix: In praise of the virtuous woman (31:10–31)

Let's read the first seven verses:

The proverbs of Solomon son of David, king of Israel: for gaining wisdom and instruction; for understanding words of insight; for receiving instruction in prudent behavior, doing what is right and just and fair; for giving prudence to those who are simple, knowledge and discretion to the young—let the wise listen and add to their learning, and let the discerning get guidance—for understanding proverbs and parables, the sayings and riddles of the wise.
The fear of the Lord is the beginning of knowledge, but fools despise wisdom and instruction. (Proverbs 1:1–7)

According to this text, what are the Proverbs for (at least for five things)?

Make up a problem.
Let's form up to seven teams with the adolescents. Each team will choose a collection of proverbs and will choose three proverbs from that collection. We must invent a problem, a situation where the proverb we have chosen will help us to make a good decision. Then each team chooses the best one and they share it with all the others.

Do you dare to tweet, put on your Facebook, Instagram, or other social network any of the Proverbs that we worked on during this session? Let's do it!

Important questions, important decisions

Proverbs is a book to live by. Without wisdom, we will almost always make poor decisions in our daily life. This is why it is very important to study this book, and even memorize the proverbs that are most useful to us.

What kind of proverbs would you like to memorize? What topics would be most useful to you? For example, relationships with friends, finances, time management, making decisions, family. . .

What about Jesus?

Jesus is God's wisdom, his Word among us. His words are still relevant today. His life is the best prayer ever made. If you want the wisest advice, the best you can do is to know Jesus and become like him.

Decide

I decide to examine God's advice, and live it in practical terms in my life, because without his advice, without his Word, I don't have enough wisdom to make the right decisions. Jesus, help me to live Proverbs 1:7: "The fear of the Lord is the beginning of knowledge, but fools despise wisdom and instruction." I will memorize it.

 To pray is a good decision. Take time to pray before dismissal.

 Remember to download the daily readings, For Depth and Applications, from www.e625.com/lessons.

Lesson 12 > ECCLESIASTES AND SONG OF SONGS

The preacher and the lover

According to your group, its dynamics and characteristics, we recommend that you focus primarily on one of these two books, Ecclesiastes or Song of Songs, and look at the other more from a bird's-eye view. But you can also prepare to study both. Pray and decide for yourself. May God give you wisdom and love!

Download at www.e625.com/lessons the complementary material for this section.

Ecclesiastes

Introduction

Ecclesiastes (*Qohelet*, "the preacher") is an extremely sincere discourse. It is a reflection on the purpose of life. Things don't always go as we expect, and it is difficult to define the purpose of life. It seems that everything is vanity (vain), that life does not make sense. Is that true? Are the thoughts we find in this book sincere? It seems to be the flip side of the coin, compared to Proverbs: sometimes things do not go well for those who are good.

What do you think of that statement?

We get very good advice: how to enjoy life and every moment of it fearing the Lord. That means, respecting him. Ecclesiastes wants us to dive into the meaning of life, taking into account everything that happens and who we are.

Division and structure

The Preacher's Experience (1:1–2:26)

What does it mean when we say that something doesn't make sense (Ecclesiastes 1:1–11)?

Why do you believe we are here? What are we born for?

In chapter 2:

What does the preacher do? Why?

In this passage, the preacher presents the problem but not the solutions. We must make adolescents understand that this is many people's reality, and that without God, any decision is meaningless. This is the proposal: let's make them want to discover the conclusion at the end, rather than stay with chapter 2.

Do you know friends who have done something similar, who have experimented to see what life is all about? How have they done it?

The preacher's ideas regarding human existence and behavior (3:1–12:8)

Many ideas are developed in this section:

In chapter 3 the preacher tells us that everything has its time (3:2–8).

And in chapters 4, 5, and 6 he develops concepts such as the development of work, not making commitments lightly, and the vanity of life.

Read Ecclesiastes 5:4–5. What does this mean? When are we in danger of it happening to us?

Sometimes adolescents make decisions, verbalize them, but are not consistent in their actions. Encourage them to think and reflect well before making hasty decisions and committing themselves. Let's give them examples.

From chapter 7 onwards the preacher returns to the concept of wisdom that he will develop until the 12th chapter.

Read Ecclesiastes 9:10. What does this verse encourage us to do? Is that wise? What would it be to do the opposite?

> *Read Ecclesiastes 11:9–12:8.*

What is this text trying to teach us?

Lesson 12 > Ecclesiastes and Song of Songs

 Let's form two or three teams to study the text and find practical advice for our friends. How would we say it in our own words? Then we can share them.

Conclusion (12:9–14)

In verses 13 and 14 we find the conclusion of the entire speech.

 What is it? Does it remind you of Proverbs, which we studied last week? Why?

Song of Songs

"The best song of all, the most sublime poem". That would be the meaning of the title of Song of Songs, which is actually a compendium, a collection of love songs.

For centuries it has been given different interpretations: the Jewish people saw it as a book that celebrates the joy of spouses united by a couple's love, and also metaphorically describing the love of God toward his people.

In Christianity, it was also understood as the love of God, of Jesus (the boyfriend) for the church. But these interpretations—although valid—should not make us forget that, in the end, this is a collection of love songs for couples, because God is the God who is love, he is the God of love, even the God of couples' love.

 What do you think God thinks of couples love? Is it good, is it bad? What does this depend on?

This book of the Bible even talks about sexuality.

 Do you think God cares about our sexuality? Why?

The book of Songs of Songs is very graphic, as it talks about kisses, compliments, etc., always within the context of mutual commitment.

 Let's take advantage of this session to talk about the importance of purity, that the Lord is in love with us, that the Gospel is essentially a love relationship, and also about how we should take care of each other, and take advantage of being single to please God. Let's remove the concept that sexuality is bad, and propose to live it in a healthy way in the light of the Word.

Division and structure

After the title and verse 1, the Song of Songs is divided into six songs according to this structure:

- First song (1:2–2:7)
- Second song (2:8–3:5)
- Third song (3:6–5:1)
- Fourth song (5:2–6:3)
- Fifth song (6:4–8:4)
- Sixth song (8:5–14)

In the last song we find this verse that is used in many engagements and weddings:

Place me like a seal over your heart,
   like a seal on your arm;
for love is as strong as death,
   its jealousy unyielding as the grave.
It burns like blazing fire,
   like a mighty flame. (Song of Songs 8:6)

How would you define love? What is the greatest love we can show another person?

What does it mean that he wears it like a seal on his arm?

The idea is to transmit a permanent love, a commitment. You can link it to Ecclesiastes 5:4–5, and point out how sometimes in this area of our lives, we make hasty decisions in our adolescence that later will have consequences (remember to always focus on mercy when discussing this topic).

If you continue to develop this theme, you can connect it with 1 Corinthians 13, to expand on the characteristics of love.

Important questions, important decisions

What do we learn from Ecclesiastes and Song of Songs?

What has caught your attention the most?

Which book do you like more, Proverbs or Ecclesiastes? Why?

Lesson 12 > Ecclesiastes and Song of Songs

What about Jesus?

Jesus is the great preacher who showed us that the most important thing is respect and love for God and love for others (our neighbor). He is the boyfriend who is looking for his bride, the church, the who falls in love with her and who gives his life for her, and who teaches us that committed love is true love.

Decide

I decide to reflect on the purpose of life. I understand that what is important is respect for God, and that what apparently many people have as a priority in life is vanity.

Regarding love, I recognize that it is something that God has created and it is great to be able to experience it at the right time. I want to dignify what God has created (my sexuality), to be wise, and be able to enjoy everything that God offers me to the fullest.

 To pray is a good decision. Take time to pray before dismissal.

 Remember to download the daily readings, For Depth and Applications, from www.e625.com/lessons.

Lesson 13 > OBADIAH AND JOEL

Obadiah

Obadiah means "servant of God." It is the shortest book in the Old Testament, with only twenty-one verses.

He writes during a critical situation: Israel had been destroyed, and recently also Judah, the Southern Kingdom, and its capital Jerusalem had fallen under the Babylonian Empire. Jewish war refugees fled to the territory of Edom (Edom is another name for Esau).

Who is Esau?

Download at www.e625.com/lessons the complementary material for this section.

Obadiah writes to Edom (they did not want to help their Israelite brothers). The lack of hospitality and love for their neighbors will be their condemnation.

> As you have done, it will be done to you; your deeds will return upon your own head. (Obadiah 1:15)

Do you know the golden rule?

Let's read Matthew 7:12.

What does this text mean?

Division and structure

Its structure is simple:

- Humiliation of Edom (1–14)
- The day of the Lord and the judgment of the nations (15–18)
- The exaltation of Israel (19–21)

Apparently, Edom was unwilling to help "his brother" during a time of great need, and this was a serious offense. Like Edom, many of us are so secure in our own lives, and are so concerned about our own things, that we don't see the needs of others.

Lesson 13 > Obadiah and Joel

In which parts of the world do you think great injustice is happening, and we or other nations are not doing enough?

The central point is for adolescents to see the importance of compassion toward others, toward those who are different, and that we have a social burden, while remembering that the most favored by Jesus are those who are last.

There is a well-known passage, a parable of Jesus, that reminds us of this situation, and is similar to the verse of Obadiah's judgment of the nations (read Matthew 25:31–40).

In what way will the king value those on the right and the left? Why?

Let's focus on the idea that compassion for others is the key to living, that what matters to the king is how we treat others, to such an extent that he even says:

> "You did it for me" (Matthew 25:40).

Sometimes it is easy to talk about how "countries" do things wrong, but what about us? Do we have compassion for our neighbors in small things?

What are practical things that we are not doing today for our neighbor, our brother, our friend, etc. due to lack of compassion?

Finally, Obadiah ends on a hopeful note:

> "And the kingdom will be the Lord's." (Obadiah 1:21).

He will one day bring justice to all those who experience injustice, but today we must be his representatives and bring that hope to our neighbor.

Joel

Before Obadiah's message to Edom, God also warned Judah of what might happen to them if they did not repent; that is the book of Joel. Using the metaphor of a plague of locusts that devastates everything, Joel will speak of the dangers that hang over the people. He will always leave a door open, because it is a warning to allow them to react. We know that in the end they will not listen, but even so, Joel contains promises from God that, despite everything, he will continue to pour out for his people. So much so, that there is a well-known text of Joel used in the first preaching by the church in the book of Acts.

Do you know what text it is (Joel 2:28–32)?

Joel was probably from a priestly or at least pious family, and his name means Jehovah is God. In his prophetic book, Joel warns the people that if they continue to make bad decisions, the consequences will be "The day of the Lord."

Division and structure

- What the locust will do (1:1–2:2a)
- New announcement about the day of the Lord (2:2b–11)
- God's mercy (2:12–27)
- The outpouring of the Spirit of the Lord (2:28–32)

You can stop here to talk about how the promise of the coming of the Spirit upon all flesh was fulfilled in Acts 2. Although the people were not faithful, God was faithful.

Judah was destroyed, but still God remained faithful.

Beyond our wrong decisions, there is a God who continues to want to "pour himself on us."

Is this a license to sin?

Let's talk about how we are responsible for our actions, but God's mercy is always there above our actions.

What do these verses demonstrate about God's character?

Judgment on the nations (3:1–16) and deliverance of Judah (3:17–21)

Lesson 13 > Obadiah and Joel

What about Jesus?

Jesus will focus on those who are last, on the disinherited; for him they will be the first.

Jesus is the one who will bring his kingdom, as told in Obadiah. We also see the fulfillment of his word in Acts 2, when the Holy Spirit came upon all flesh. Despite our rejecting Jesus, he was declared Lord and to have his Spirit live in me.

Decide

I decide to get to know God and his interests, not being apathetic to the needs of my neighbor. I decide to follow Jesus and to be filled with him, have his presence and invoking his name to be saved.

 To pray is a good decision. Take time to pray before dismissal.

 Remember to download the daily readings, For Depth and Applications, from www.e625.com/lessons.

Lesson 14 > HOSEA AND AMOS

Hosea

I don't know if we are ready for this story: God asks Hosea to marry a prostitute. She will be a symbol of what God's relationship with his people is like, and also of our relationship with him.

 Why do you think this image can describe our relationship with God?

Time after time Gomer, Hosea's wife, makes bad decisions. So do God's people, who will eventually be conquered by Assyria.

Gomer then abandons Hosea, but God asks the prophet to return to her, to redeem her.

Hosea's life becomes his message.

Gomer's infidelities are a reflection of how we act; yes, we have God, we pray and all that, but just like the people of Israel, we also have "other gods" with whom we adulterate.

God wants exclusivity, like a husband, like a wife. With nobody else. In this text this story is mixed with Hosea's prophecies, and we see ourselves reflected, both in our mistakes and in the unconditional love of God.

 Download at www.e625.com/lessons the complementary material for this section.

Division and structure

 Print the structure by downloading it from www.e625.com/lessons.

 Looking at the structure, what do you think Hosea's central teaching will be?

Hosea's marriage will be an example of God's relationship with his people.

Lesson 14 > Hosea and Amos

 Download the comparative table from www.e625.com/lessons and make two teams to complete the picture with the biblical text.

HOSEA AND GOMER	GOD AND ISRAEL
Hosea marries Gomer 1:3	God marries Israel 2:19
Hosea is faithful 3:3	God is faithful 1:7
Hosea is not reciprocated 3:1	God is not reciprocated 3:1
The relationship breaks 3:1	The relationship breaks 2:2
Gomer seeks other men 3:1	Israel seeks other gods 4:1
Gomer shows indifference 3:1	Israel shows indifference 11:1
Hosea's daughter: unloved 1:6	God will not pity His capricious children 5:6
Hosea's other son: Lo-Ammi ("not my people") 1:9	God declares that the Israelites are not His people 1:9
Hosea restores Gomer 3:2	God redeems unfaithful Israel 14:4–8

Important questions, important decisions

What is exclusivity in relationships? Why is it important?

Do you think we should be exclusive for God? Why?

What other gods are there competing for our hearts and decisions (mental map, picture, etc. . .)?

Amos

Amos said of himself that he was neither a prophet nor the son of a prophet, but he certainly prophesied (he spoke in the name of God). This simple man from the countryside spoke mostly of the injustices that were being committed in the Northern Kingdom, Israel, by the rich toward the poor. He also denounced the inequalities and the sins of seven of Israel's neighboring nations.

His message is so powerful that even today civil rights lawyers continue citing his texts.

Division and structure

- Introduction (1:1–2)
- Prophecies against the nations (1:3–2:16)

Look for the texts and determine what the accusations are, and what their bad decisions are.

Download the list of nations from www.e625.com/lessons.

- Damascus: war crimes
- Gaza: sold slaves, deported the Jewish people
- Tire: same as Gaza, and also breached a peace treaty
- Edom: fought against the Jews
- Amun: genocide against the Jews
- Moab: desecrated the corpse of the king of Edom
- Judah: disobeyed God's law
- Israel: social injustice

Do you think God cares about social injustices? Why?
- Judgment on Israel (3:1–15)

- Israel's stubbornness (4:1–5:27)
- Lament for the unjust (6:1–14)
- Three visions of disaster (7:1–9)
- Amos confronts Amaziah (7:10–17)
- Vision of the end of Israel (8:1–14)
- Vision of the sovereign God at the altar (9:1–10)
- Promise of future restoration (9:11–15)

Throughout the Bible God insists on one thing that his people must do: help the defenseless and the weak (read Amos 9:11–15). The end of Amos tells us that God will restore the house of David, and that it will be something for all nations.

As always, the prophets finish with some words of hope that point to a future where everything will be restored, despite the injustices.

Important questions, important decisions

What do you think God would denounce today, of all that is happening in the world with the nations?

What can we do today for those who are last?

What about Jesus?

Jesus is the husband who, in spite of our infidelities, continues to demonstrate his grace and love. Even if we deceive him and we are unfaithful, like Gomer was, he redeems us and forgives us. He is also the promised son of David who will bring justice in the midst of injustice to all nations, and the one who continues to care for the least of us.

Decide

I decide to be exclusive for Jesus and to not deceive him with other gods. I decide to be concerned about and take care of those who are last, and to not tolerate the injustices that I find along the way.

To pray is a good decision. Take time to pray before dismissal.

Remember to download the daily readings, For Depth and Applications, from www.e625.com/lessons.

Lesson 15 > ISAIAH

A great Gospel in the Old Testament

Isaiah is the prophet who most explicitly speaks of the Messiah, seven hundred years before the birth of Jesus!

The New Testament authors quote this book about fifty times, and with good reason: Isaiah's words and prophecies are full of confrontation, warnings, and exhortations but also of hope and the fulfillment of promises, especially pointing to the Messiah who will save the people. It also offers apocalyptic sections, the story of King Hezekiah, and many evocative images. It's quite a work of art, written from Jerusalem.

This book was read by Jesus himself at the synagogue of Nazareth (Luke 4:17–19), confirming that those words were being fulfilled in him.

Download at www.e625.com/lessons the complementary material for this section.

> Read Luke 4:17–19.

What did this text mean to Jesus? Did he fulfill what was written there? How?

This text is Jesus' statement of purpose: his identity was anchored in the Scriptures, the Word of God.

It is full of poetry focused on the Messiah, knowing that he would be the suffering servant who would come in weakness and be rejected. So precise was Isaiah that some call the book of Isaiah "the fifth Gospel".

The prophet speaks for three different times, well differentiated in their structure.

Division and structure

Print the structure by downloading it from www.e625.com/lessons.

Let's take a bird's-eye view at the division and structure, since it is very long and dense. Teens can keep it to study, but you can highlight the most important points that we suggest, and also those that you consider relevant.

There is a well-known text that continues to attract attention today for the precision with which it describes Jesus, the Messiah who will appear in the New Testament, and it is known as the "suffering servant passage." Read Isaiah 53.

Print the text of Isaiah 53 so that, in groups of three, the teens can study the text and associate it with the person of Jesus, to see how each of the predictions that Isaiah makes is fulfilled.

In the middle of the twentieth century, some manuscripts of Isaiah from 100 years before Christ were found in Qumran, near the Dead Sea, which demonstrates the authenticity of the facts.

After seeing all this information, what do you think of this prophecy?

If Jesus is the fulfillment of this prophecy, how does this affect my life?

If Jesus is who he said he is, this has to change everything that we are. We have to feel forgiven and justified, and we have to learn to live not for ourselves but for him.

What about Jesus?

Yes, Jesus will be that servant who suffers, and who dies to save us all. Isaiah, like the whole Old Testament, points to Jesus as its complete fulfillment.

Decide

I choose to believe that Jesus is the fulfillment of Old Testament prophecies, that he is the salvation of the world, and also my salvation, and that through him I am justified and forgiven.

To pray is a good decision. Take time to pray before dismissal.

Remember to download the daily readings, For Depth and Applications, from www.e625.com/lessons.

Lesson 16 > NAHUM, HABAKKUK, AND ZEPHANIAH

Maybe you can choose two of these three prophets for this session, as it will be more educational. If you are interested in the content of all three, you can treat these books more from a bird's-eye view.

Download the three structures that you will find in www.e625.com/lessons.

Nahum

One hundred years before Nahum, Jonah had gone to preach in Nineveh, although at first he did not want to go. The result was the repentance of the Ninevites.

But this time it will not happen: Nineveh is about to fall, and Nahum is the prophet who will speak to them about what is going to happen to them. Finally Assyria, the first international empire, believing themselves to be very powerful, was going to be destroyed because of its sins, war crimes, and idolatry.

They were a particularly cruel people, known for their terror methods to punish their enemies. They sowed fear wherever they went and, despite the Lord's warnings, they did not change their ways.

Download at www.e625.com/lessons the complementary material for this section.

Division and structure

- Psalm of praise for the vengeance of the Lord (1:1–2:2)
- Prophecies regarding coming judgment on Nineveh (2:3–3:19)

What will happen when we put our trust in our own strength to make decisions? Will we always get away with it?

What can happen if, after many warnings, we fail to obey and act in accordance with God's wisdom?

Habakkuk

This prophet lives in Judah, and knows that the people are not doing what's right, but he does not want God to erase them from the map, but to correct them.

He knows that the Babylonians are going to punish the Jews, and he cannot believe that God is going to use the Babylonians, knowing that they are even worse. But God assures him that the Babylonians will get what they deserve.

This book is not properly speaking a message addressed to the Jews; it is rather a conversation between Habakkuk and God, a prayer.

Habakkuk does not like God's answer, and continues talking to him, asking him questions: "For how long…?" In a heartfelt way, the book continues, and ends with words of trust in God's will through a song that is one of the most moving and tender statements of faith in all of Scripture. It reminds us a bit of the book of Job, who challenges God but ends up placing his trust in him.

In addition, one of the verses from this book will become the foundation of one of the most well-known letters in the New Testament.

Do you know which one?

"But the righteous person will live by his faithfulness." (Habakkuk 2:4)

Why do you think this verse will be the foundation of the letter to the Romans?

The idea is to emphasize that the letter to the Romans is an exaltation of God's grace above all circumstances. Trust and faith in God is what makes us righteous, not our moral perfection. This verse from Habakkuk is the seed that the apostle Paul will use for his letter to the Romans that has blessed the world so much.

Division and structure

- Habakkuk's first complaint (1:1–4)
- God's first answer (1:5–11)
- Habakkuk's second complaint (1:12–2:1)
- God's second answer (2:2–20)
- Prayer-song of Habakkuk (3:1–19)

This is what the last part of the song says:

> Though the fig tree does not bud
>   and there are no grapes on the vines,
> though the olive crop fails
>   and the fields produce no food,
> though there are no sheep in the pen
>   and no cattle in the stalls,
> yet I will rejoice in the Lord,
>   I will be joyful in God my Savior.
>
> The Sovereign Lord is my strength;
>   he makes my feet like the feet of a deer,
>   he enables me to tread on the heights.
> (Habakkuk 3:17–19)

❓ How would you explain this text in your own words?

In the midst of adverse circumstances that we do not understand, the natural reaction is to complain. We see many things as unfair and we blame God. It's good for us to be sincere before him, but it is even better to trust in him unconditionally, because if we don't, we can make bad decisions based on pain or rancor. We read about a song of joy and happiness, based not on the circumstances but on the God who sets free.

Let's learn to "sing," to live that way.

Zephaniah

We now come to one of the most overlooked books of the Bible. (You won't have heard many sermons from Zephaniah.) The main point of this book is that God will give the Jews one last chance to repent, and if they don't take it he will destroy their nation, or even the entire world. Even so, afterwards God promises to restore the people. Taken out of context, it looks like a book written by a doomsayer, someone who predicts evil and almost takes pleasure in doing so, but this warning paid off. The time was between 640 and 621 bc when Josiah, king of Judah, ascended the throne at the age of eight! His father Amon had done evil in the eyes of Jehovah, but Josiah, the new king, at age sixteen, discovers the Book of the Law and recovered the faith of his ancestor David.

Thus he initiated a cultural reform, tearing down the pagan sanctuaries, and at age twenty-three he renovates Solomon's temple. It appears that Zephaniah transmitted his message of warning during the early years of Josiah's reign, and it was heeded.

Lesson 16 > Nahum, Habakkuk, and Zephaniah

Have you ever been warned about the consequences of making a bad decision? Did change your mind?

You can think in advance of an experience of your own as an example to share with the group, to facilitate participation. Keep it short!

Let's look at the structure of this book.

Print the structure by downloading it from www.e625.com/lessons.

Important questions, important decisions

Do we see a pattern in the writings of the prophets?

Does this structure resemble that of the prophets we have studied previously?

The idea is to show that many of the prophets were denouncing the situation in which the people found themselves, and warning of the dangers of disobeying God, and of its consequences. They were calling for repentance, for a change in who they were and what they were doing, and they would end with words of hope, often independently of what they chose to do.

You can look at the structure of other prophetic books studied up to now and see the parallels. You can do it in groups, individually, or all together, depending on the time you have left in your session.

This is how Zephaniah ends:

> "At that time I will deal with all who oppressed you.
> I will rescue the lame;
>   I will gather the exiles.
> I will give them praise and honor
>   in every land where they have suffered shame.
> At that time I will gather you;
>   at that time I will bring you home.
> I will give you honor and praise
>   among all the peoples of the earth
> when I restore your fortunes before your very eyes,"
> says the Lord.
> (Zephaniah 3:19-20)

Like a good shepherd, God will gather his sheep again, even though they are lost. Thus ends this text, with these words of hope-as the words of the prophets often do. And we know to whom they were pointing.

What about Jesus?

Jesus is the word of hope and restoration, despite the misconduct of his people. It is in him that we place our trust "though the fig tree does not bud". Let us not put our trust in our own strength, like the Ninevites did, but in the Lord, knowing that "the righteous person will live by his faithfulness."

Decide

I decide to listen to the Lord's warnings in my life, knowing that he always seeks what's good, what's best for me, even if I do not understand everything. He will be my song in the midst of my difficulties, and the hope in my life.

To pray is a good decision. Take time to pray before dismissal.

Remember to download the daily readings, For Depth and Applications, from www.e625.com/lessons.

Lesson 17 > EZEKIEL AND DANIEL

Prophets away from their home

Ezekiel and Daniel were two prophets who ministered away from their home, mostly in Babylon. Ezekiel, a deported priest, jobless and turned prophet, and Daniel, a young expatriate who will serve at court.

Like them, we are surrounded by people who do not know the Lord, but God asks us to bless them, to live in their midst. Let's remember that we are not "home" yet. We are foreigners, and we must be with the people but at the same time make a difference. We must be like Ezekiel and like Daniel: the voice of God in any situation.

Download at www.e625.com/lessons the complementary material for this section.

Ezekiel

The prophet Ezekiel preached to the exiles in Babylon. (He was also an exile, from 593 to 571 bc)

The Babylonians had not captured the Jews to enslave them, but to displace the population of Israel—especially its leadership—expecting that in this way they would lose their identity as a people, and mix with the Babylonians. Perhaps there is no better way to "finish off" a people than by making them forget who they are.

 How would you get a people to lose their identity?

 How do you think the world tries to make us lose our identity?

In this book, Ezekiel speaks in many ways to convey the message: through poetry and prose, proverbs, parables, puns, allegories, lamentations, etc.

The central purpose of his book is to bring spiritual renewal to all people. He wants them to return to a true worship of God. "May they know that I am the Lord" (this phrase is repeated sixty-five times in the book).

At the end, as always, we will be told that God, although he has allowed exile, will restore his people.

Division and structure

- Prophecies against Judah and Jerusalem (1:1–24:27)
- Prophecies against foreign nations (25:1–32:32)
- Prophecies concerning Israel (33:1–39:29)
- Vision of the new temple and the new law (40:1–48:35)

Many images from Ezekiel are well known: the valley of dry bones that come to life, the bad shepherds and the good shepherd, the glory of the Lord leaving the temple, the four creatures that pull the chariot of God (which some will interpret as the four evangelists). It is a book full of symbols, inspiration, and creativity, from one of the most visually oriented prophets of all.

Daniel

A young man who was also deported to Babylon during the time of Nebuchadnezzar, and who was also a prominent prophet. Not only that: he became an adviser to Nebuchadnezzar and also to other Babylonian and Persian kings. He knew how to be faithful to God in the midst of an environment that pushed him to deny God. Daniel and his three friends (Shadrach, Meshach, and Abednego) paid a price for remaining apart for God while at the same time forming part of the social fabric of the time.

They were like us: we are in this world, even though we are not of this world. Our call is to be a blessing to those around us but at the same time maintain our identity as followers of Jesus, so we will face many pressures and we will have to learn to make wise decisions within our society.

In the story of Daniel there are two very different sections: a narrative, where the story of Daniel and his deported friends is told (chapters 1 through 6) and a prophetic and apocalyptic section (chapters 7 through 12).

In chapter 1 we are told about how Daniel and his three friends lived differently in order to not become contaminated, despite being in a very difficult situation.

In chapter 2, Daniel interprets Nebuchadnezzar's dream and in chapter 3 we are told about how they suffered in the fiery furnace for not bowing their knees to worship an idol, and how they were rescued.

In chapter 4 we are told the story of Nebuchadnezzar's madness, and how he regains his sanity. In chapter 5 Daniel interprets the writing on the wall during Belshazzar's feast, and in chapter 6 Daniel passes the test of the lions' den.

Lesson 17 > Ezekiel and Daniel

 Make six teams, one for each chapter to be discussed (if there are less than twelve people you can reduce the number of chapters used, it is not necessary to cover them all).

The task of each team is:

1- *Read the text.*

 2- *Download the text from www.e625.com/lessons for work teams.*

3- *Answer these questions:*

- What problem is presented to the protagonists?
- What would be the consequences of not deciding wisely?
- What did the protagonist(s) do?
- What were the consequences of their decisions?
- What can we learn from them for today?

4- *Expose it briefly to the others.*

The last chapters (from 7 through 12) are prophecies that speak of the end times, the son of man, and other apocalyptic images that inspired many of the New Testament authors.

Important questions, important decisions

 What have we learned from the lives of Daniel and his friends?

 Do we face similar situations for defending our faith? What are they?

What about Jesus?

Jesus will be the good shepherd of Ezekiel, the son of man to whom authority is given, the one who will restore his people, the rock that will topple kingdoms, the king who rules over all kings.

Decide

I decide to make a difference in a place that is not mine, in my Babylon, to be a true blessing to others, even if they do not yet know Jesus. I decide to prepare myself like Daniel and his friends to be excellent at what I do and to maintain my identity in Christ wherever I am.

 To pray is a good decision. Take time to pray before dismissal.

 Remember to download the daily readings, For Depth and Applications, from www.e625.com/lessons.

Lesson 18 > JEREMIAH AND LAMENTATIONS

"Jeremiah, the weeping prophet." This is how they have called the author of these two books, written around the same time as Zephaniah, Ezekiel, and Habakkuk. Jeremiah's calling began at a young age, perhaps when he was thirteen years old! He saw with his own eyes the fall of Jerusalem and he mourned over it.

In both Jeremiah and Lamentations, Jeremiah shows us his own inner struggles more graphically than any other prophet. It is not always easy to follow God and his words, and Jeremiah is an example of this.

 Download at www.e625.com/lessons the complementary material for this section.

Jeremiah

As the main point of his message, the prophet Jeremiah will denounce not a social issue, an injustice, or the mistreatment of others, but the fact that the people have abandoned God and have placed their trust in idols.

(Read Jeremiah 2:10–13.)

For forty years Jeremiah will be ministering by warning the inhabitants of Jerusalem about the consequences of abandoning God. They will ignore his voice and will lock him up, but still Jeremiah will try to convince them through different methods (such as the example of the clay pot that we will look at later). Finally the city will fall into the hands of the Babylonians.

 Pass out Play-Doh or other material that can be used to mold and make figures, and challenge the group to make a piece of art titled "Me at My Best."

Division and structure

- Introduction (1:1–3)
- Jeremiah's call (1:4–19)
- Covenant dispute: the sins of Jerusalem and Judah (2:1–24:10)
- Jeremiah as a prophet to the nations (25:1–51:64)
- Appendix: the fall of Jerusalem (52:31–34)

In the introduction and the call we see the following verses:

> (Read Jeremiah 1:4–8.)

 Do you believe that the Lord has called you to do something for him and for others?

Jeremiah was going to face great challenges and had to make very tough decisions, in accordance to his call.

 How are the clay figures going?

An example of the type of prophecies and symbols that Jeremiah used to communicate his message is found in chapter 18.

> (Read Jeremiah 18:1–6.)

 Have some teens describe what they wanted to "mold" with the Play-Doh. Have them pass it to the person next to them, and now. . . they have to undo it. Sometimes we build things that appear to look good, but then we need to redo them. Although it hurts God like it hurts us—we are his creation—he wants us to be the best we can be, the best version of us, and sometimes he has to undo in order to rebuild. This was what happened with the people of Israel. Jeremiah pointed them to the future when God would restore them, but he had to "break his work" to do it again.

 Have we felt in our life that our mistakes and bad decisions have led us to have to start over?

 **Are we willing to put ourselves in God's hands so that he can form what he wants in us?**

 With the shapes that we have now, invite them to rebuild.

Lamentations

 Can you share what has been your saddest moment?

As on other occasions, you can share an example from your life.

The focus is that sadness is a legitimate feeling when things are not going well, and that the Bible understands those circumstances, but nevertheless in the midst of them we must continue to trust, like Jeremiah.

Lesson 18 > Jeremiah and Lamentations

This is probably the saddest book in the Bible. Its structure is a chiasmus, that is, it has a central axis that is the important part, and is surrounded by themes in parallel form, backwards and forwards (an ABCBA type structure, where C is the main theme). It is a very common structure in Hebrew literature, and both the Old and New Testament have plenty of them.

Division and structure

- Lamentation after the destruction of Jerusalem (chapter 1)
- Personal suffering after the destruction of Jerusalem (chapter 2)
- Hope in the face of adversity (chapter 3)
- Grief over the destruction of Jerusalem (chapter 4)
- A reminder that God still reigns (chapter 5)

As we see, it begins with weeping. Chapters 1 and 5 summarize the siege and fall of Jerusalem.

Chapters 2 and 4 bring up more explicit and personal details about the devastation, and chapter 3, the center of the chiasmus, moves between regret and hope.

It's like climbing a mountain and coming back down, and at the very top is hope.

Seeing this structure, what would be the theme of Lamentations?

We can see how a superficial study can be misleading, but looking at the structure we realize that, in the midst of so much tragedy, the prophet continues to communicate one message: hope.

Another detail of this work of art is that the first four chapters are an acrostic composition; in the original, each verse or group of them begins with a letter of the alphabet (as if today we were to begin the first sentence with A, the second with B, and so on).

Isn't it amazing how these authors worked on their text?

Even in a text as heartbreaking as Lamentations there is still room for creativity, order and composition that greatly enrich biblical study, because the Bible is a fascinating book. Do not weep so much if your own shape has been destroyed, or it has not turned out as well as you had hoped. You will have a new opportunity. Take it home and take advantage of this week's devotionals to build and mold it again in the best way that you can.

Important questions, important decisions

What have we learned from Jeremiah and Lamentations?

Can we identify ourselves with this prophet? Why?

What can we decide today in our lives to allow it to be molded by God?

What about Jesus?

In Jeremiah, Jesus is the shepherd who will come (Jeremiah 23), the king who will reign and will make a new covenant. In Lamentations, He will be the afflicted Messiah, who feels our pain, who reminds us of that wonderful text from Isaiah 53.

Decide

I decide to accept my calling, no matter how old I am. I know that God wants me to serve him and to be a voice in the midst of my own situation. I decide to stand firm in the decisions that I make in light of His Word, and to trust in Jesus even in the saddest moments.

To pray is a good decision. Take time to pray before dismissal.

Remember to download the daily readings, For Depth and Applications, from www.e625.com/lessons

Lesson 19 > HAGGAI AND ZECHARIAH

Finally good news!

Haggai

After seventy years of Babylonian exile, the people of Israel return to Jerusalem. Cyrus, the new king of Persia, issues an edict that allows the exiles to return to the promised land. Behind them are the prophets who warned about what was going to happen. Now is the time to rebuild Jerusalem and its temple. But not everything is rosy. Many of those who have returned care only about themselves, and neglect the temple that was in ruins. That's why Haggai came, but with an optimistic and encouraging focus. In fact, Haggai means "festive" and his work was to encourage the people to work on the restoration of the temple. It is likely that he was an old man; His ministry was short-barely four months-but it was very significant to the people.

Zerubbabel—the governor who was appointed at that time, a descendant of David—and Joshua—the priest—were encouraged by these new prophets to restore Jerusalem into what it once had been. Haggai, who perhaps remembered what the temple had been like, and seeing that people were caring only about their own things, encourages and exhorts them with these words:

> (Read Haggai 1:4—8)

Download at www.e625.com/lessons the complementary material for this section

The people were showing indifference toward God's things. . .

Do you think this is happening today? Are we into our own things and not into God's?

How would you define God's things?

Haggai encourages them, as well as us, to reflect about our priorities, reminding them that the Lord is with them (1:13) but telling them not to put their own well-being above worship.

This is Haggai's message.

Think about this sentence:

> "If you don't have time for God, you live wasting your time."

 What do you think it means? How would you apply it to your life?

If your decisions are based only on your own interests, you won't get past yourself and you won't get involved in what God wants from you. Haggai encourages us to celebrate the opportunity we have of becoming involved in the restoration of this world, of God's people, of his church.

The people had delayed the time for the rebuilding, it never seemed like it was the perfect time.

This also happens to us, but remember: Not making a decision is already making a decision. Many of us do not make a decision to get baptized, or to undertake something that we know we should, and as time passes, it becomes more difficult to start. Isn't that so?

 You can give a personal example to illustrate this last paragraph.

Division and structure

- The call to rebuild the temple (1:1—15)
- Indifference (1:1—11)
- Repentance (1:12—15)
- The greatest time and the greatest blessings from God (2:1—23)

The last part is also very encouraging. There is a verse from this short book that's mentioned a lot in the churches:

> 'The silver is mine and the gold is mine,' declares the Lord Almighty. 'The glory of this present house will be greater than the glory of the former house,' says the Lord Almighty. 'And in this place I will grant peace,' declares the Lord Almighty. (Haggai 2:8—9)

Do you remember from last week what was destroyed? Well, God confirms that the second masterpiece will be better than the first one. God is an expert in rebuilding our lives. It doesn't matter if we are ever in ruins; God wants to restore us.

The temple will finally be rebuilt, and many years later Herod will expand it, and it will be larger than the first one. And none other than Jesus will attend that temple.

Zechariah

"Jehovah remembers," that's what Zechariah means. Zechariah is, a prophet with a different feel from the previous ones, who ministered to the exiles who had returned to Jerusalem, and brought them a message of hope: the God who remembers his people in his mercy.

In this book Zechariah encourages the people to turn to the Lord to be cleansed of their sins and experience his blessing, and he also brings words of comfort and encouragement for the rebuilding of the temple.

He describes a series of visions in which he remarks that God is with his people. He also deals with various topics, and the last part is more apocalyptic.

Division and structure

- Call to repentance (1:1–6)
- Zechariah's visions (1:7–6:15)
- A question about fasting (7:1–8:23)
- An oracle about the nations and Israel (9:1–11:17)
- An oracle about the future of Israel (12:1–14:21)

Other than the great Isaiah, Zechariah brings us, in just fourteen chapters, more prophecies about Jesus than any other book from the Old Testament.

 These verses from five hundred years before Christ pointed to Jesus. Let's look at the texts in teams of two or three people, and look to see what parts of the life of Jesus they are connected with. (At the end, we will invite some representatives from the groups to present their findings.)

- Zechariah 9:9
- Zechariah 11:13
- Zechariah 12:10
- Zechariah 13:7

Important questions, important decisions

What do we learn from these prophets and their new way of preaching?

Why was Haggai's message important?

The whole BIBLE in a year for HIGH SCHOOL

 What does that message motivate us to do today? How do we apply it to our lives?

What about Jesus?

Jesus appears in an obvious way in Zechariah, chapter 14. He will be the coming judge, the just king, who will give us salvation. In Haggai he reminds us that the last glory will be greater than the first, and all this will be fulfilled in Jesus.

Decide

I decide to dedicate myself to God's business and not put my own comfort ahead of his purposes. I decide to set aside time for God, and accommodate my priorities to him.

 To pray is a good decision. Take time to pray before dismissal.

 Remember to download the daily readings, For Depth and Applications, from www.e625.com/lessons.

Lesson 20 > ESTHER

The Old Testament novel

We find ourselves in Persia. King Ahasuerus has succeeded his father, Darius the Great. If we were to summarize this novel, we would say something like this: it is a palace plot where we will see a Jewish orphan who wins a beauty contest become the king's new wife, and later, with help from her cousin Mordecai, will save her people from genocide. To remember these events, the Purim festival is established, which to this day continues to be celebrated in Israel.

Esther is a book where God is not explicitly mentioned, but we see his hand caring for his people.

Download at www.e625.com/lessons the complementary material for this section.

Do you know what providence is?

The concept is that God acts in our midst even if we don't see it. God works in this world through us, our stories, and our decisions.

If we were aware that God works in the world through our decisions, what would we change today in our actions and thoughts?

Have you experienced God's providence in your life?

Division and structure

In this session it is important for the adolescents to have their Bible, so they can follow the thread of the story.

Queen Vashti is dethroned and Esther becomes the new queen (chapters 1 and 2)

King Ahasuerus offers a banquet to his guests, and at the end of the party (which lasted several days) this happens:

> (Read Esther 1:10–12.)

Queen Vashti refuses to attend the party, and the king's advisors counsel him not to see her again. In a male chauvinist society as they had at the time, they feared that women would have the same rights as men.

But even in the midst of this injustice, God acts.

(Read Esther 2:2—in the NIV—and then Esther 2:5–7.)

Finally, after an authentic beauty contest and twelve months of preparation, Esther was selected queen, but she hid the fact that she was Jewish.

Haman's plot against the Jewish people (chapters 3 through 7)

Haman, an advisor of the king, was exalted above the others and everyone knelt before him, but Mordecai did not, and this angered Haman.

(Read Esther 3:5–6.)

Haman manipulated the king into making a decree to annihilate all the Jews, in exchange for 330,000 kilograms of silver (about two hundred and forty million dollars!).

The liberation of the Jewish people (chapters 8 and 9)

Upon finding out about the plot (chapter 4), Mordecai pleads with Esther to intercede for them before the king. Esther, her attendants, and all the Jewish people fasted for her for three days. Risking her life because she could not appear before the king unless he called her, she presented herself to Ahasuerus, and he held out his scepter to her in approval.

If you were Esther, how would you feel? Would you believe that you were born for that day, to save an entire people? What thoughts would go through your mind?

Do you think it was a wise decision? Why?

(Read Esther 5:4.)

Haman, who had conspired against the Jews, does not know what the situation; he still wants to destroy Mordecai and prepares a gallows to kill him.

Often there are people who do not wish us well.

Lesson 20 > Esther

How do you think we should act?

The focus is that we should not take revenge on our own, but trust in God's providence.

During the second banquet in which they are together, the king asks Esther what is on her mind and why she wanted to see him. Then she tells him:

(Read Esther 7:3–6.)

Haman is discovered, and gets a taste of his own medicine on the gallows he had prepared for Mordecai (quite a poetic twist, as this story draws to a close). Although the previous edict of the king was irrevocable, he dictates new laws to allow the Jews to defend themselves, and others to help them, and in this way they were able to protect themselves from extermination.

This is what happened, and they established the festival of Purim to remember that they were freed from this "holocaust."

Exaltation of Mordecai (chapter 10)

(Read Esther 10:1—3 to see how the book ends.)

The story ends in celebration and joy. It's a story in which the name of God is not mentioned, but there is no doubt that God was behind the scenes, directing the steps of his people.

Important questions, important decisions

Do you believe that God is behind your life, directing your story? Why?

What can we learn from Esther's attitude? And from that of Mordecai?

What about Jesus?

Jesus, like Esther, came for "this hour" (Esther 4:14), to save his people and to enable us to celebrate that he has set us free.

Decide

I decide to trust in God's providence, and to be aware that he does his will through my free decisions.

 To pray is a good decision. Take time to pray before dismissal.

 Remember to download the daily readings, For Depth and Applications, from www.e625.com/lessons.

Lesson 21 > EZRA AND NEHEMIAH

The project: rebuild the city

Cyrus decree in 539 B.C. made it possible for the Jews to return to Jerusalem from exile. From that moment, the people started returning to their land, which was in ruins. The prophets encouraged them to build the temple and repopulate the city. There was enthusiasm in the air, but it was a very big project. Life is a very big project.

Ezra and Nehemiah will be two of the most important leaders of that time, in order to build not just the walls or the temple but also the hearts of the people.

The project is huge. To see how the return and reconstruction happened, look at this diagram:

Download and print the diagram of that time from www.e625.com/lessons.

The return from exile happened in three phases (with permission from the Persians):

- First group: Zerubbabel (538 BC) began to rebuild the temple (Ezra 1—6)
- Second group: Ezra (458 BC) with many reforms (Ezra 7—10)
- Third group: Nehemiah (444 BC) rebuilt the wall (Nehemiah 1—6)

In the Hebrew Bible, Ezra and Nehemiah are combined into one book. Some scholars tell us that the author of both books is Ezra, the priest and scribe, who compiled all the information from that time. We must understand them as one unit: one without the other will be incomplete.

Do we have a project for our lives? Do we know the decisions we must make to "build" it? How long is it going to take us?

During the study of these two books we will see the importance of the reconstruction project in two aspects: that of the city, and that of the people of the city. Both are important, and complement each other like the books of Ezra and Nehemiah.

Ezra
Division and structure

Return of the first group of exiles and reconstruction (1:1–6:22)

Let's read Cyrus decree (Ezra 1:2–4).

This decree was extremely important for the Jewish people, since it was the key that allowed them to return to their land. It is a historical document that marked the course of God's people.

In this section we see many lists of names of people who returned with Zerubbabel, as well as legal documents, and the first constructions and reconstructions. Also in chapter 4 we see opposition—as always happens when someone starts a project—and we will see this in more detail in Nehemiah. Thank God that Haggai and Zechariah (remember them?) keep encouraging the people to rebuild the temple until they succeed.

Return of the second group of exiles and Ezra's reforms (7: 1–8: 36)

In this second section we find Ezra and his genealogy (very important, to show that he met the conditions to be a priest).

In chapter 9 we are told about how Ezra leads the people spiritually. It's not only the external works that are important, but also the construction of the heart. At the end of this book we see Ezra's interest in maintaining the purity of the people (their emblem and identity) to keep the destruction of the city from happening again.

Many times in our life's journey we pay attention to external things, such as what to study, how to dress, what to own, and we do well to build all of that. But we must not forget that what sustains our lives is what is not seen: our hearts.

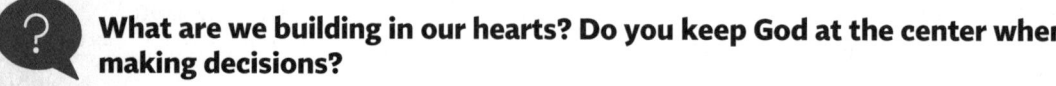

What are we building in our hearts? Do you keep God at the center when making decisions?

What is more important: the construction of the exterior or the interior? Why?

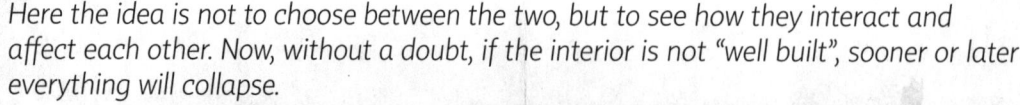

Here the idea is not to choose between the two, but to see how they interact and affect each other. Now, without a doubt, if the interior is not "well built", sooner or later everything will collapse.

Lesson 21 > Ezra and Nehemiah

Nehemiah

He was the cupbearer of King Artaxerxes (a high post in the Persian Empire) in Susa, the capital. He was Jewish and Jerusalem was in his heart. Shortly after the events of the book of Ezra, God ignited his heart to continue with the rebuilding project, especially Jerusalem's wall—which was miraculously completed in just fifty-two days. In the text of Nehemiah we will see how the rebuilding was carried out, and what we can learn to build our own life in accordance with what God wants for us.

Depending on how much time you can dedicate to this part, you can focus on reading a verse from the structure or do a bird's—eye view of the chapters to follow the sequence of events.

Division and structure

Rebuilding the walls of Jerusalem (1:1—6:19)

- Nehemiah's prayer (1:1—11)

Seeing the need, the first thing Nehemiah does is pray. Yes, pray; something as simple as talking to God. Before planning, making decisions, or thinking about what to do, Nehemiah prays.

Praying is what comes first, but it is what comes first.

When you want to make a decision, do you pray first? Why?

Why do we use prayer as a last resort, instead of the first?

What consequences does it bring?

Nehemiah's plans (2:1—20)

Here in Jerusalem, after studying the city walls, Nehemiah will devise a plan of action, not improvise. Sometimes we think that improvising is the most spiritual thing we can do, but it is not. When we have a clear strategy it is easier to make decisions within that framework. If we have a clear goal, we can determine if the decision that we are making helps us get closer to that goal or not.

Nehemiah's work (3:1—32)
For this reason, in chapter 3, he distributes the work by families, according to his strategy, and each of them makes their contribution to the total construction.

Opposition to reconstruction (4:1—23)
But not everything will be smooth sailing. Samballat, an enemy of the people, conspires to keep them from finishing the job, so the people must take precautions.

When we have a plan or a project and start working on it, external threats will usually come (people or difficulties that will try to prevent us from finishing the work). We must count on it happening and adapt to it. Perhaps you want to study to get ready for a specific career, or to serve God in a specific area, but unexpected difficulties may come along the way, and you must learn to adapt and not get discouraged. Maybe it's a sign that you're on the right track!

The Jews began to post guards to protect themselves from this external threat.

The people's conflict inside Jerusalem (5:1—19)
But alas! There was also conflict and arguments within the city about what was fair for one group or for another. (Sometimes if external threats do not paralyze us, internal weaknesses.) But Nehemiah took charge of these matters, and resolved the conflict by providing justice.

We also suffer from these types of weaknesses. When there is a team project, sometimes internal conflicts are more difficult to resolve than outside threats. And if you have an individual project, your own sin or discouragement can derail your project.

What dangers do you see in the lives of people that can leave their projects half done? And in your life?

Give an example of your own. You know how it works

Renewed opposition (6:1–19)
Sanballat does not give up and falsely accuses the Jews to intimidate them. Sometimes criticism or slander will come into our lives, but we must not give up. Quite the contrary, we must stand firm and endure until the end.
Let's not answer with the same coin: let's put all of this before God in prayer, as Nehemiah did.

(Read Nehemiah 6:14–16.)

Restoration of the Jewish community (7:1–13:31)

- Registration of the people (7:1–73)
- Revival with Ezra (8:1–10:39)
- Repopulation of Jerusalem (11:1–12:26)
- Dedication of the walls (1:27–47)
- Restoration of the people (13:1–31)

The wall was finished, and then different events took place that celebrated what had happened with God's help: a registration of the people is made and Ezra reads the law in front of everyone with renewed courage they confess their sins and the pact is restored, new priests and Levites are instituted, and Nehemiah finishes some additional works to improve the city.

We must celebrate the accomplishments that we achieve together, and we must not forget that in the end it is all accomplished by the grace of God.

It's great to see how this book ends. After everything Nehemiah has done, he continues to recognize that God is the one who continues to help him.

> *Remember me with favor, my God. (Nehemiah 13:31b)*

Nehemiah's Process

PRAYER	PLANNING	DANGERS	FINAL CELEBRATION
		External Threats	
		Internal Weaknesses	
		Criticism	

The whole BIBLE in a year ⟶ HIGH SCHOOL

 Download at www.e625.com/lessons the complementary material for this section.

 Write your own life project for the next five years, at a spiritual, emotional, professional, etc. level. Write a sentence, a plan. What do I want to build? Make a list of internal and external difficulties that you may encounter, and describe how you will celebrate your achievement, following the example of Nehemiah. Keep this in your Bible as a reminder.

 Download the Me in Five Years activity from www.e625.com/lessons for teens to work on.

Important questions, important decisions

What can we learn from Ezra and Nehemiah?

What has caught your attention the most?

What motivates you, from this lesson, to make changes or decisions?

What about Jesus?

Jesus will leave his position—just like Nehemiah—to restore his people, face opposition, and invite us to build his kingdom with him. Like Ezra, Jesus will remind us of his law and help us keep it.

Decide

I decide to make plans in fear of God, seeking his purpose for my life, and taking care not only of my external projects, but also of God's project in my heart, as he wants to restore me and make me like Jesus.

 To pray is a good decision. Take time to pray before dismissal.

 Remember to download the daily readings, For Depth and Applications, from www.e625.com/lessons.

Lesson 22 > MALACHI

His name means "My Messenger." These will be the last words of the Old Testament: it will end on a question mark, with an open ending. (In fact, the last word of the Old Testament is "curse" or "destruction." Not a very good ending, is it?)

The people have already settled in Jerusalem and resumed their practices. While it is true that the Jews no longer worship idols, they are not without other dangerous behaviors:

1. They are offering diseased and injured animals (there is neglect and spiritual indifference). People offer sacrifices religiously but not from the heart; they don't really care. Moreover, the priests tolerate such behavior.

2. There are still intermarriages with women who worship idols (they no longer care about purity).

3. They do not tithe, and by not doing so they not only fail to comply with a mandate but also demonstrate the people's greed and selfishness by not wanting to invest in the common good. They benefited, they consumed spirituality, but they did not want to make the commitment to bless others.

4. There was social injustice, oppression of the poor, and deprivation of justice for the homeless.

How would these types of dangerous behavior apply in our context today?

Examples: offering imperfect animals would be like us not giving God our best, going to places only when he interests us, not having spiritual disciplines, and only paying attention to God when we think we need him.

So we see a working system, where people show up but have lost their essence, a religion without content, without heart, where things are done by inertia.

This may be the case for many of us, who may be part of the system but perhaps we are doing things just to do them. We are being apathetic or hypocritical in our behaviors and decisions, giving God the leftovers and not placing him where he deserves to be: at the center of our lives.

How would you define hypocrisy?

The whole BIBLE in a year FOR HIGH SCHOOL

 Hypocrisy is a word that comes from the Greek, and means "actor." When a Greek actor would put on a mask, he was a "hypocrite." Sometimes we find ourselves wearing masks—even Christian ones—supposedly doing the right thing, but we are only acting.

 Do you think this is a dangerous behavior that can affect us today? How?

In this book we see the messenger raising a series of "controversies" to get God's people to reflect. Let's see if he makes us reflect as well.

 Download at www.e625.com/lessons the complementary material for this section.

Division and structure

- Controversy over God's love (1:1–5)
- Controversy with the priests over honoring God (1:6–2:9)
- Controversy over the infidelity of the people (2:10–16)
- Controversy over God's judgment (2:17–3:6)
- Controversy over returning to God (3:7–12)
- Controversy over rebellion against God (3:13–17)
- Warnings about the coming of the great day of the Lord (4:1–6)

Spiritual indifference

In some parts of Malachi we see the people questioning God with expressions that reflect their broken heart.

 Find the suggested texts and complete the table available at **e625.com/lessons**. In groups of two or three teens, have them read the contexts of the verses, looking for the problem, and for what we can ask ourselves today. (Use the first one as an example, if you think it will help.)

1. *How have you shown us that you love us (1:2)?* This speaks of a lack of trust in God, because they were arguing that he had not been faithful.
Application: Do we think that God is not being faithful to us?

2. *When have we showed contempt for your great name (1:6)?*
Defiled ritual sacrifices, you say? When have we done such a thing (1:7)? This speaks of reluctance and indifference. They were just doing the proper thing.
Application: Do we offer from the heart our whole life to God? Or do we merely comply with the rituals?

3. *We have never disobeyed your instructions (3:7)! This speaks to us of a terrible blindness to their own sin.*
Application: When faced with our own sin, do we make excuses?

4. *When have we stolen from you (3:8)? This speaks of the selfishness and greed of the people.*
Application: Do we joyfully offer our lives and resources to God?

5. *What have we said against you (3:13)? This exposes the insensitivity of the people.*
Application: Do we serve God wholeheartedly?

The end of this book (and therefore of the Old Testament) is enigmatic:

> "See, I will send the prophet Elijah to you before that great and dreadful day of the Lord comes. He will turn the hearts of the parents to their children, and the hearts of the children to their parents; or else I will come and strike the land with total destruction." (Malachi 4:5–6)

The book ends with the wait for the Messiah, and it says that before he comes, Elijah must return. (As you may know, Elijah did not die, and the Jews believed that he would return to point to the promised Messiah. Read Matthew 11:14.)

What does this text tell us?

In the end, even though there are some words of hope, there is no resolution. It's as if there's a second part that is missing. The Jews are still waiting for the Messiah, but we have already found him. We know how to answer the question that the Old Testament asks us.

Important questions, important decisions

What have we learned from Malachi?

Do we see, when examining our own lives, a shallow and empty spirituality? To what extent or in what way do we see it?

What about Jesus?

Jesus will be the answer to the question posed by the last Old Testament prophet: God will send "his messenger" to announce Jesus. John the Baptist, the expected Elijah, will point to Jesus and say: "Look, the Lamb of God, who takes away the sin of the world!" (John 1:29).

Decide

I decide not to live a superficial spiritual-appearing life. I don't want to just be part of a designed system and only do what I'm supposed to do. I want to live wholeheartedly and with all my strength for God, and to keep trusting in him.

 To pray is a good decision. Take time to pray before dismissal.

 Remember to download the daily readings, For Depth and Applications, from www.e625.com/lessons.

Lesson 23 > HOW ARE THE OT AND THE NT DIFFERENT BUT COMPLEMENTARY?

We come to the hinge point that divides the Bible into two: the Old Testament and the New Testament. They are obviously two different sets of books, but do they present different gods? A God who in the OT was a judge now becomes all love and forgiveness? Is there continuity or discontinuity in the history of salvation?

Why do you think the Old Testament is important?

What is the biggest difference between the two Testaments?

> *"Do not think that I have come to abolish the Law or the Prophets; I have not come to abolish them but to fulfill them"* (Matthew 5:17). Jesus did not come to abolish the law, but to fulfill it.

What does this verse mean?

The New Testament will be the fulfillment of the Old Testament. In Jesus, the prophecies of the prophets will make sense and the law will be fulfilled, and what was seen as a shadow now comes to light. Jesus is the key to interpreting the Scriptures.

Some people believe that the Old Testament and the New Testament speak as if they were talking about different gods, or about the same God but one that has changed his mind.

Why do you think they believe this?

Let's lead the group to understand that the God of Scripture is the same God yesterday, today, and always, that the questions that arise in a timely manner regarding the character of the God of the OT have an answer, and that all Scripture is fulfilled in Jesus.

Do you remember any of the books of the Old Testament, and how they pointed to Jesus?

Between the last prophet (Malachi) and the beginning of the New Testament, four hundred years passed, known as "the silence of God". This is not because God did nothing—he is always acting even when we do not see it—but it marks for us a before and an after that will change history forever.

Division and structure

 Download the structure of the New Testament from www.e625.com/lessons.

The NT begins with the four Gospels, four points of view of the life of Jesus, his deeds and sayings, his life, death, and resurrection.

This is followed by the second part of one of the Gospels: Luke writes the book titled the Acts of the Apostles, the history of the early years of the church, beginning in Jerusalem and ending in Rome, the capital of the empire.

Then come a series of letters or "epistles" (letter in Greek), written by authors like Paul of Tarsus, who will write to communities of faith in different cities and will also write personal letters—like Philemon's—and some like the so-called "pastorals," 1 and 2 Timothy and Titus. Then comes the epistle to the Hebrews (author unknown) and the epistles written by James, Peter, and John.

Finally, we will find a brief letter from Judas and the book of Revelation. The New Testament opens the map where the events occur, toward the West.

The Roman Empire will be the backdrop where all the acts of the early Christians will take place, inspired by the man from Galilee who changed the world. The story will not only be that of the Jewish people, but it will be the fulfillment of Genesis 12:3: "Through you, I will bless all the peoples of the world," a promise God made to Abraham.

 **If you know them, what is your favorite New Testament book? Why?**

 Encourage the group to memorize the order of the books of the New Testament. It is important to remember them in order to know where to find them. You can joke with the fact that now we all use our cell phones to read the Bible, but that can make us more dumb, like when we use the calculator even to do simple maths. Again, encourage them to use their physical Bibles, underlining parts of them, taking notes, etc.

The Old Testament is a shadow of the New Testamen; it is its precursor. The New Testament is the Old Testament's fulfillment. One without the other is incomplete. We cannot understand the sacrifice of Jesus without knowing the history of Israel. And the Old Testament, when read from the perspective of Jesus, makes much more sense. Each of its pages is illuminated by Jesus light.

Lesson 23 > How are the OT and the NT Different but Complementary?

Also, many people have their own interpretations, but the correct and most accurate interpretation is the one of the author. That is why Jesus said: "You know it's written in the law... But I tell you...".We must learn to read and interpret the Old Testament from the point of view of Jesus.

Read Luke 24:13—35 in three voices: narrator, Jesus, and disciples, for a touch of humor. Be sure to have them exaggerate it.

When Jesus rose from the dead, he approached two disciples who were going home discouraged. They didn't recognize him, but Jesus went through all of Scripture, teaching them something.

What was he trying to show them (v. 23)

Does it agree with what we have seen in the previous Old Testament sessions? Why?

How were their eyes opened?

Important questions, important decisions

What have we learned from this introduction to the New Testament?

Can one Testament be understood without the other?

What about Jesus?

Jesus is the fulfillment of all Scripture; everything studied so far points to him. Now we will see how he appears in history and transforms it forever.

Decide

I decide to discover the person of Jesus in all of Scripture, so that the passion for God will burn in my heart.

To pray is a good decision. Take time to pray before dismissal.

Remember to download the daily readings, For Depth and Applications, from www.e625.com/lessons.

Lesson 24 > THE GOSPELS: MARK

An action story

In these first lessons about the Gospels we will see that each of them places a different emphasis on the person of Jesus. For this reason, we will not study the entire content of all the Gospels, but rather the most important details and the unique contributions that each of them makes to the narrative of the most important story ever told. Let's make our adolescents become passionate about Jesus through these windows that, from different points of view, bring us closer to him.

Although it appears as the second book in the New Testament, the Gospel of Mark was written first. Mark was a disciple of Peter.

His name was John Mark, and he appears several times in the book of Acts (and also in some of the letters from Paul and Peter). It's interesting to see that he didn't make the best decisions at first, but he finally became helpful.

Mark is mentioned in Acts 15:37–39; Colossians 4:10; Philemon 11; 1 Peter 5:13; and 2 Timothy 4:11.

If we read all these texts, how can we perceive that it was John Mark?

He was the one who started a new literary genre: the Gospel, "the good news"; the Gospels of Luke and Matthew were inspired by it. Much of Mark's text is also found in these two Gospels, and they have a very similar perspective, which is why these three books are known as the "Synoptic Gospels" (Greek meaning same vision or point of view).

Download at www.e625.com/lessons the complementary material for this section

The Gospel of Mark is not a biography, it does not start with a genealogy like the other two, and it does not have the great speeches, like the Sermon on the Mount. Mark is a reporter who narrates the news of what is happening, the story of pure action orchestrated by Jesus.

It is the shortest of the Gospels and it is intense. In it we will see Jesus acting, doing things all the time. If the Gospels were rivers, Mark would be a river full of rapids, ideal for rafting. He reminds us more of Jesus deeds than of his words, although

Lesson 24 > The Gospels: Mark

there are also teachings of Jesus. It is basically a Gospel of the facts of the Jesus of action, the one who performs miracles, who heals and transforms.

Why do you think that what Mark remembers the most are the actions of Jesus?

Division and structure

Basically Mark is divided into two parts, and we could see it as a mountain that goes up from chapter 1 to 8 and comes back down from there to chapter 16.

Download the mountain structure of Mark for the teenagers to complete with the titles.

Prologue (1:1–15)
- Preaching of John the Baptist, precursor of Jesus (1:1–8)
- The beginnings of Jesus' ministry (1:9–15)

1. Jesus the Messiah, the King (1:16—8:30)
- Acts and teachings of Jesus (1:16–3:12)
- Proclamation of the kingdom of God (3:13–6:6)
- Jesus reveals himself as the Messiah (6:7–8:30)

2. Jesus, the Son of Man (8:31–16:20)
- Jesus announces his death (8:31–11:11)
- Jesus' activities in Jerusalem (11:12–13:37)
- Passion, death and resurrection (14:1–16:20)

These are guide verses. Now narrate the story quoting the ones that you choose.

Prologue (1:1–15)
Preaching of John the Baptist, precursor of Jesus (1:1–8)

This introduction is apotheotic: it introduces us to John, a prophet in the desert, wearing strange clothes.

> And this was his message: "After me comes the one more powerful than I, the straps of whose sandals I am not worthy to stoop down and untie. I baptize you with water, but he will baptize you with the Holy Spirit." (Mark 1:7–8)

Imagine that you did not know that he is talking about Jesus with that message. What would you think the one he is describing is like?

The beginnings of Jesus ministry (1:9—15)

Jesus is baptized by John and is tempted by Satan in the desert. After passing the test, he chooses some of his disciples.

1. Jesus the Messiah, the King (1:16—8:30)
- Acts and teachings of Jesus (1:16—3:12)

Immediately his ministry begins.

 In groups of two, make a list of everything Jesus did (miracles, etc.). We end up tired from reading about so much movement!

- Proclamation of the kingdom of God (3: 13—6:6)
 Then Jesus chooses his twelve apostles and begins teaching.

 In groups of two, make a list of Jesus teachings and his deeds.

 What do people understand as success? Why do you think people followed Jesus?

We see Mark remembering more the acts than the words of Jesus. Today people are tired of mere talk; we must not only speak, but also act. In Mark's Gospel we see Jesus being consistent with his message.

 What does being consistent mean?

Let's guide the teenagers to understand the importance of having their acts become consistent with their words. A perfect speech is of no use if our lives do not reflect the values that we preach.

 What do we call those people who say one thing and do another? How can we avoid behaving like that?

- Jesus reveals himself as the Messiah (6:7—8:30)

In this section Jesus continues to teach and perform miracles. There are many well-known texts: the feeding of the five thousand, Jesus walking on the water, etc., and this section ends at a summit, on the top of the mountain of our story, the middle, the epicenter of the text (read Mark 8:27—30).

Lesson 24 > The Gospels: Mark

The Christ, the Messiah, the one everyone was waiting for, the fulfillment of the Scriptures! Everything is looking up, a man who works miracles and teaches like no one else. "This is the person we've been waiting for!" they were saying to each other.

But perhaps he will not meet all expectations, because from this very point we move on to the next section. He will no longer be just the Son of God, he will also be the Son of Man.

2. Jesus, the Son of Man (8:31—16:20)

Why do you think that Jesus is not only the Son of God but also the Son of Man?

- Jesus announces his death (8: 31—11:11)

In 8:31 Jesus tells us that he has to suffer much and die on a cross. He no longer presents himself as the triumphant leader, but as someone who has come to serve. In this section the transfiguration appears, a sublime moment, but Jesus will announce his death three times.

What do you think is easier: to follow the Jesus who was going up, or something that's going down?

In 10:17—27 Jesus tells us the famous story of the rich young man. Do they know it?

Let them tell it, or read it.

Like us, this young man wanted to follow Jesus, but there was a problem.

What was it?
In his case, it was his wealth, his material success. Following Jesus will always be of blessing, but it comes at a price. Many of us have impediments to following him.

Why is it hard for us to follow Jesus?

Many times his plans are not ours, he changes our plans; We cannot use our own criteria to follow him. The path is not always going up, but if we follow Jesus wherever he takes us, it will be the right path.

- Jesus' activities in Jerusalem (11:12—13:37)
Upon reaching Jerusalem, everything accelerates even more. Jesus arrives triumphant, but then he overthrows the tables of the money changers in the temple, and they conspire to kill him.

In 12:28—31 we find what Jesus considers to be the most important commandments.

Why do you think these are the two most important commandments?

- Passion, death and resurrection (14:1—16:20)

Finally, Jesus is arrested, tried, denied by Peter, sentenced to death, crucified, and then dies and is buried.

But then we receive the news that changes everything: he is risen!

The king who came, the Messiah who went downhill, who came to serve and to die for all of us, has risen.

God saves us through his sacrifice; and not because of his greatness, but because he became like us. He is not only the Son of God; he is also the Son of Man.
Mark finishes his Gospel with a message of hope for humanity: Jesus came to show us that death does not have the last word.

Important questions, important decisions

If the news that Mark wanted to tell us is true, how does it change things? How does it affect my life? Is this just another piece of news, or is it the best news we could have ever been given? Why?

What about Jesus?

In Mark's Gospel, Jesus is the Son of God, the Son of Man, the King, the Messiah who came to die for us and who rose again to bring us hope.

Decide

I decide to follow Jesus (whether he takes me uphill or downhill), and if there are things today that prevent me from following him, I decide to put them aside. I decide to be consistent with my acts, because words and speech are not enough.

To pray is a good decision. Take time to pray before dismissal.

Remember to download the daily readings, For Depth and Applications, from www.e625.com/lessons.

Lesson 25 > THE GOSPELS: LUKE

The story of Jesus, the stories of Jesus

Luke is a unique Gospel, and is actually the first part of a history in two volumes: Luke and the Acts of the Apostles. It's good to know that Luke is the only non-Jewish New Testament author (probably from Antioch in Syria).

He was a Gentile, like us, a doctor who accompanied Paul on some of his trips. This is the most human Gospel, and it presents Jesus above all as the Savior (of all of us, not just of a specific people group).

These two volumes—one third of the New Testament—were written for a pagan named Theophilus, who wanted to know the history of Jesus and of the church. Like us, he will discover Jesus in this text as the Savior of the whole world.

This Gospel contains some of the most unforgettable stories of Jesus, such as the story of the prodigal son and the story of the good Samaritan.

Can you tell one of these parables from memory? What do we learn from them?

It is interesting that we can remember better the stories than the rules. The "simple" parables of Jesus contain life principles that changed history forever.

What is a "parable"? What characteristics do they have? Why did Jesus teach through parables?

Unlike Mark, Luke will be more extensive and will include teachings of Jesus where we can delve into his speeches, and many of them will be parables, unique stories that will only appear in this Gospel.

Today we are used to talking about Jesus as our Savior, and we owe that to Luke.

In Matthew and Mark the word savior does not appear even once, and in John's Gospel it appears only once (John 4), but in Luke's it appears frequently.

Why do you think this is?

One third of the book is unique and has no parallel in the other three Gospels. Chapters 9-19, which tells of the road to Jerusalem, will be filled with stories that remind us how to live "on the way" as Jesus did.

In this Gospel we will find Jesus closest to us, and at his most human. "The Son of Man."

Division and structure

This is the structure of the Gospel of Luke, which is divided into five parts.

 Download from www.e625.com/lessons the five parts of the Gospel of Luke, Print them so they are able to take notes.

Introduction to John the Baptist and Jesus (1:1–2:52)
This section tells us about the birth of John the Baptist and of Jesus, and is full of songs: Mary sings, Zechariah sings (prophesies), and even the heavenly hosts sing.

 Identify in groups of two or three people where these songs are found and study their content. What do they want to communicate? What is the reason they are sung?

 You can make three different groups so that each one studies one of those songs.

 Remember to keep track of time. If it will take them too long to do this exercise, just mention it. The focus of this lesson will be studying the parable of the prodigal son.

Preparation for ministry (3:1–4:13)
Here we learn of the ministry of John the Baptist, and how he baptizes Jesus. In 3:23–38 we see the genealogy of Jesus (in Matthew we also see it but it only goes back to Abraham, and in Luke it goes back to Adam, because Jesus is not only the savior of the Jews but of the whole world, of all the children of Adam).

Then we have the temptation of Jesus in the desert (more detailed than in Mark), and immediately afterwards his ministry begins.

Ministry in Galilee, the revelation of Jesus (4:14–9:50)
In 4:16–19, in the synagogue, Jesus reads a text from Isaiah 61, and says that it talks about him; it is his declaration of intentions.

According to this text, why did Jesus come?

Can we make this declaration of intent our own? How?

Remember to connect to Isaiah's lesson, and how it already pointed to Jesus.

What does it mean that Jesus has come for the sick and not for the healthy?

In this section of the Gospel there are miracles, casting out of demons, etc., the introduction of some parables and teachings, and the feeding of the crowds. John the Baptist is executed and Peter confesses that Jesus is the Christ, the Son of God (9:20). Jesus then announces his death, is transfigured on Mount Tabor, and again announces his death, although the disciples do not understand it.

Journey to Jerusalem, the Jews' rejection and a new way (9:51—19:44)

In this section Jesus begins his journey to Jerusalem and here we find many of the unique teachings in this Gospel. Here there are many disagreements with the Pharisees, and those who try to eliminate him; Jesus also teaches about prayer (the short version of the Lord's Prayer appears in Luke 11) and we are told about the price of following him.

Finally, we come to one of the high points of the New Testament: the parable of the prodigal son, in Luke 15.

 Read the parable of the prodigal son (Luke 15:11—32).

Luke 15 has three parables told to the two types of people we've mentioned before. They are very similar stories, with a similar structure:

1. Something is missing
2. Somebody goes to look for it
3. He finds it
4. The result is joy

 Download at www.e625.com/lessons the complementary material for this section.

Everyone knows this story of a father and his two sons, where the youngest son wastes everything but comes to his senses and approaches home appealing only to his father's mercy. In this story we are shown the heart of Jesus for the lost.

The whole BIBLE in a year - HIGH SCHOOL

What is your favorite verse from this text?

Which character in this story do you identify with the most?

What was the prodigal son's problem? And what was the problem of the older brother?

Make two teams, that of the older brother and that of the younger brother, and each one of them—based on the text—makes a list of good and bad decisions that each one made, respectively. Then they share them with the whole group.

Which of the two is better?

The idea is that neither of them is better, but in the end, the younger brother is at the feast, while the older one hasn't yet made his decision.

Download the sheet for both teams.

Many leave home but others stay but fail to experience the love of the Father. This can be a very important topic for the teenagers in the group. The majority may be children of believers, used to the "Christian" environment, to being at home like the older brother, but without enjoying God as a daddy. Use pastoral sensitivity when dealing with this issue.

Take advantage of the fact that the emphasis in Luke is that Jesus is the Savior. It doesn't matter how far or how close you are from home. The important things are if the Father has embraced you, you have recognized your error, and you recognize Jesus as your Savior. This section may be important for adolescents and their decision to not just "be around" but to follow Jesus.

In Jerusalem, Jesus is executed and is resurrected (19:45–24:53)

Arriving in Jerusalem, Jesus purifies the temple (19:45–48) and that will be the final trigger for those who want to kill him. He will be arrested in chapter 22. Finally, in this fifth section, Luke narrates the death of Jesus. As a doctor, he gives many important facts about Jesus' suffering.

Why did Jesus suffer so much? Was it just physical pain?

Lesson 25 > The Gospels: Luke

Here you can spend some time with verses that narrate what Jesus went through for us, and how his sacrifice was made out of love, to save us. Some verses that you can use are 22:63–65; 23:33, 36, 46.

Chapter 24 is a good ending: the resurrection. "Why do you look for the living among the dead? He is not here; he has risen!" (Luke 24:5—6).
Jesus is not found among the dead, but among the living. The resurrection is our great hope, and it confirms that Jesus' decisions were the right ones.

The decision to know the Father and to live for him does not lead to death, but to life, hope and eternity, and the resurrection confirms it.

Important questions, important decisions

Of the two groups that appear in the Gospel of Luke—Pharisees and teachers of the law on the one hand, and sinners and tax collectors on the other— which do you identify with the most?

What do you think is the main idea about Jesus that Luke wants to convey?

What is most important to you in this lesson?

What about Jesus?

Jesus is the Savior and this Gospel reminds us of that fact over and over again. Jesus is the Savior of the whole world, and he also wants to be your Savior.

Decide

I decide to acknowledge Jesus as my Savior. His resurrection is the proof that he was right. I decide to recognize that I need healing in my heart, and because Jesus came for the sick, then I invite him to heal and save me.

 To pray is a good decision. Take time to pray before dismissal.

 Remember to download the daily readings, For Depth and Applications, from www.e625.com/lessons.

The whole BIBLE in a year for HIGH SCHOOL

Lesson 26 > THE GOSPELS: MATTHEW

Matthew is the Gospel of the community, of the church; in fact, it is the only Gospel where this word appears. Here we don't only have the action as we do in Mark, but it is mixed with teaching passages, such as the Sermon on the Mount, the parables, etc. It has a very pedagogical structure (see below) to strengthen the concepts about Jesus that the author wanted to convey. Not only the acts of Jesus, but also his words, the teachings of the Master. In this Gospel the word "church" appears in verse 16:18 and in chapter 18 (in the other three Gospels it does not appear at all).

The importance of the community and of what we must learn in it has more weight in this Gospel than in the others.

Why is the church important? What does it contribute to us? What do we contribute to it?

Matthew, Mark and Luke are called the "Synoptic Gospels" (same optics, same point of view) because they are very related to each other and share a lot of material, despite the fact that each one of them places a different emphasis on the person of Jesus, which is so rich in nuances.

Everyone knows the Great Commission; that is found at the end of the Gospel. There we see some of the last words of Jesus to his disciples, and they are also very important for us today. We must decide in this lesson if we will also make his mission our own mission, or if we will disregard the mission that Jesus has designed for this world.

Do you think that Jesus left a mission for us to accomplish? What is it? How can we carry it out?

In this lesson we want to tell the adolescents:

- that they should have a life project, that they should decide to follow Jesus' life project, which is the Great Commission, by being his disciples and following his teachings.
- that the life of Jesus should be an example of a life with meaning, with purpose.
- that God is not only something extra for us to add to our lives, but the designer of all that we do and all that we are.

To accomplish this, we will focus on the five sermons that appear in the Gospel of Matthew, to connect them to the Great Commission. Thus, the structure of this Gospel will encourage us to live his mission, and to decide to fulfill the Great Commission.

Division and structure

This is Matthew's structure:

1. Jesus' childhood (1:1—2:23)

(Here we have the genealogy of Jesus from Abraham; the Gospel of Matthew was intended for people of Jewish background.)

2. Beginning of Jesus' ministry (3:1—4:11)

3. Ministry of Jesus in Galilee (4:12—13:58)

    - Sermon on the Mount (5:1—7:29)
    - Mission Sermon (10:1—11:1)
    - Parables of the Kingdom (13:1—58)

4. Ministry of Jesus in various regions (14:1—20:34)
- Sermon on community life (18:1—35)

5. Jesus in Jerusalem: the passion (21:1—28:20)
- End times sermon (24:1—25:46)
- Passion, death and resurrection (26:1—28:20)

Download Matthew's five sermons and the five parts of the Great Commission at www.e625.com/lessons.

 Make five groups or teams, and give one of the sermons to each group. They have fifteen minutes to read it and see what that sermon is about by answering two questions:

What do we think is the main idea?

What application does it have for today?

Then they must connect the sermons to the Great Commission.

 These five sermons correspond to a sentence from the Great Commission. The idea is that the Great Commission condenses the teaching of the five sermons that Matthew tells us. So, we will indicate the relation of the sermons with the sentence and the explanation, to share it with the adolescents.

Lesson 26 > The Gospels: Matthew

The Great Commission (Matthew 28:18—20)

Then Jesus came to them and said,

All authority in heaven and on earth has been given to me. […]

(Sermon on the Mount, 5:1—7:29)
Jesus, like Moses, begins to teach on the mount. He is the new "lawgiver." He says: "You know that it is written in the law… But I tell you…" He is the one who will send us because he has the authority to do so. He is the one who can truly interpret the Scriptures. This earth belongs to God.

Therefore go and make disciples of all nations […]

(Mission Sermon, 10:1—11:1)
Here we are told how we should go.

Baptizing them in the name of the Father and of the Son and of the Holy Spirit […]

(Parables of the Kingdom, 13:1—58)
Jesus immerses us in stories not in order to get us to understand absolutely everything, but rather to enable us to experience it, to savor the love of God as expressed in the love of the Trinity. Baptism is an experience that submerges us so that we can be part of that story that Jesus tells us. Do we want to become a part of his parables?

[…]and teaching them to obey everything I have commanded you.

(Sermon on community life, 18:1—35)
Tells us how we should live in community, with forgiveness as its foundation, and always keeping in mind those who are lost.

And surely I am with you always, to the very end of the age.

(End times sermon, 24:1—25:46)
We must remember that the end of the mission is his return. He will come back to finish what he started. Our hope is rooted in this.

Download at www.e625.com/lessons the complementary material for this section.

Important questions, important decisions

Do you think the Great Commission was only for the disciples who were there, or is it also for us? Why?

What things would change in your life if the Great Commission became your priority?

Why do you think we don't fulfill the Great Commission?

What about Jesus?

Jesus is the Messiah, the one who was expected in the Old Testament. Matthew will constantly anchor the person of Jesus with the Old Testament prophecies, since he is the fulfillment of Scripture. The first book of the New Testament, as it appears in our Bibles, has its roots in the Old Testament.

Decide

I decide to accept the Great Commission, the charge that Jesus left to all of us who have decided to follow him.

 You can propose to the group to memorize Matthew 28:18–20 this week.

 To pray is a good decision. Take time to pray before dismissal.

 Remember to download the daily readings, For Depth and Applications, from www.e625.com/lessons.

Lesson 27 > THE GOSPELS: JOHN

Presenting the Logos

The last Gospel to be written was that of John. It is the most intimate of all, the one that shows us the person of Jesus very closely, from the inside.

To know the purpose of the Gospel of John, let's read John 20:31 which says:

But these are written that you may believe that Jesus is the Messiah, the Son of God, and that by believing you may have life in his name.

According to this text, what is the objective of this Gospel?

The purpose of this Gospel is to show us how to find eternal life, how to know and trust in Jesus, the Son of God.

What do you think is the word repeated the most in this Gospel?

The most repeated word is believe. John will give us a number of signs (seven, a number that he liked very much) with the same objective: that we may believe in Jesus, that is, that we may put our trust in him. It is not only about believing the right thing (that is, knowing the correct answers), but also about believing in the biblical sense, which is to put our trust in God.

In this Gospel we find what is perhaps the best-known verse in the entire Bible. Do you know it by heart?

For God so loved the world that he gave his one and only Son, that whoever believes in him shall not perish but have eternal life. (John 3:16)

Why do you think this is the best-known verse?

Download at www.e625.com/lessons the complementary material for this section.

Division and structure

Prologue (1:1–18)

1. Public ministry of Jesus, the Christ (1:19–12:50)
— John the Baptist (1:19–34)
— Beginning of Jesus' ministry (1:35–3:36)
— Jesus is the Christ–confrontation with the Jewish authorities (4:1–6:71)
— Jesus is the light and life to the world (7:1–12:50)

2. Passion, death and resurrection (13:1–21:25)
— The Last Supper (13:1–17:26).
This section is special for us. In it, John opens the door to the place where the last supper was held, and for five chapters he presents us with the words that Jesus gave to his disciples at that important moment. It was the last moment that Jesus would spend alone with his disciples before the passion and the cross, and what he said was profound, not to be forgotten. Before speaking, he washed his disciples' feet, an act of service and humility that would mark them forever.

We will see some things that Jesus said at that dinner.

Sit with the teens on the floor, in a circle, like they did at a first—century dinner. Have each one read a verse and together interpret what Jesus meant. You must facilitate their participation.

The words of Jesus at dinner: 13:35; 14:6; 14:15—17; 15:16—17; 16:7; 17:3; 17:15; 17:21

- Arrest, trial, death and burial (18:1–19:42)
- The resurrection (20:1–21:23)
- Epilogue (21:24–25)

There is a peculiarity in this Gospel: John will show seven signs to talk about the divinity of Jesus.

- Turning water into wine (2:1–11)
- The healing of the son of a king's official (4:46–54)
- The healing of a paralytic (5:1–18)
- Feeding a multitude (6:1–14)
- Jesus walks on the water (6:16–21)
- The healing of a man blind from birth (9:1–12)
- The raising of Lazarus (11:1–45)

Lesson 27 > The Gospels: John

Which of these signs is your favorite? Which one do you think best shows that Jesus is the Son of God, worthy of our trust?

You can choose a couple of these signs and read the passages in full. All these signs are intended for the reader to make a decision to trust Jesus, to believe in him. This is the purpose of the Gospel of John, which is why many recommend that it should be the first one to be read!

Encourage teens to take a step out in faith through these signs.

The signs are not an end in themselves, but rather point to something; in this case, the signs point to Jesus. The whole Gospel of John is about that.

> "If I want him to remain alive until I return, what is that to you? You must follow me." (John 21:22) What's important is the personal decision that we make toward Jesus, regardless of what others decide.

Important questions, important decisions

What do you think is the most important lesson in the Gospel of John?

Why is John not one of the Synoptic Gospels? How is it different from the other three Gospels?

Which is your favorite Gospel?

What about Jesus?

Jesus is the Son of God. In John Jesus is described as the Word made flesh. There is no genealogy, as John connects him directly to God. And the incredible thing about that Word, that eternal being, is that he became flesh, he became a man and dwelt among us. He made himself understandable so that we may know him and trust in him.

Decide

I decide to believe in Jesus, the Son of God, and to trust in him. Because everyone who believes in him has eternal life.

The whole BIBLE in a year ✈ HIGH SCHOOL

 To pray is a good decision. Take time to pray before dismissal.

 Remember to download the daily readings, For Depth and Applications, from www.e625.com/lessons.

Lesson 28 > ACTS 1—12

The church's Big Bang

Jesus has risen and now the church has the commission to get the Lord's message to the end of the world. We are in the second book that Luke wrote to Theophilus. In this second volume we will find the first church sharing the Gospel throughout the Roman Empire, led by some Christians. In first place Peter, then other apostles and followers of Jesus, and then the unexpected Paul of Tarsus.

Do you know who Paul of Tarsus was?

We will see his conversion and how he went from persecuting the church to becoming the apostle to the Gentiles.

The book starts in Jerusalem and ends in Rome, the heart of the empire. In this first part we will see the church in Jerusalem, and its first steps toward the Gentiles. In the second part we will delve into Paul's missionary trips, finishing with his imprisonment in the imperial capital.

God calls us to be witnesses, that will be this lesson's invitation: to be witnesses wherever we are of the resurrection of Jesus, of what he has done in our lives, and of what he can do in the lives of others.

What does it mean to be a "witness" to a fact? What is the job of a witness?

Today we are heirs of that early church, and we continue to be called to be witnesses of the resurrection. Let's see how the book of the Acts of the Apostles is structured.

Division and structure

Download the structure from www.e625.com/lessons.

- Prologue (1:1–26)
- Preaching of the Gospel in Jerusalem (2:1–8:3)
    - Pentecost (2:1–42)
    - Lives of the first Christians (2:43–5:16)
    - Persecutions (5:17–8:3)

Why did the early Christians suffer persecution?

Do Christians today suffer persecution?

Preaching the Gospel in Samaria and Judea (8:4-9:43)
Preaching the Gospel to the Gentiles (10:1-28:31)
Peter's activities (10:1-12:25)

Prologue (1:1—26)

> But you will receive power when the Holy Spirit comes on you; and you will be my witnesses in Jerusalem, and in all Judea and Samaria, and to the ends of the earth." (Acts 1:8)

And this will be the order of events: It will start in Jerusalem, then things will happen in Judea and Samaria, and finally unto the ends of the earth, with the missionary journeys of Paul and his team.

Preaching of the Gospel in Jerusalem (2:1—8:3)

Pentecost (2:1—42)

> In the Gospels we see Jesus with us, but in Acts comes the promise of God within us: the Holy Spirit. The founding text of the church is Acts 2:2—4 (read this passage aloud). This text expresses God's intention that the message reach everyone, people of every language and nation. Immediately afterwards, Peter will rise to share the first speech given by the church, a summary of Jesus' life, his death, and his resurrection. That day they added... three thousand people!

Lives of the first Christians (2:43—5:16)

Persecutions (5:17—8:3)

Why were Jesus' followers persecuted? Are there people today who suffer +persecution for the Gospel? Who?

Preaching the Gospel in Samaria and Judea (8:4—9:43)

An unexpected protagonist appears in this section: Saul of Tarsus, whom we know today as the apostle Paul.

Read the incredible story found in Acts 9:1—16.

What was Saul's life like before he met Jesus?

Lesson 28 > Acts 1-12

In verses 15 and 16 we see both sides of the coin of Jesus' call.

Show a coin to illustrate how, on the one hand, God wants us to be useful in his hands (the "heads" of the coin, verse 15), but on the other hand we must also pay a price to be his instrument (the "tails" of the coin, verse 16).

There are many who want to be and live verse 15, but not verse 16.

Why?

God calls us to change our lives and our ways to share the good news about him, which changes everything. To decide to live for Jesus sometimes implies suffering, leaving some things aside, giving up some of our rights to start living for others. Without this, the book of Acts would not have been possible.

Preaching the Gospel to the Gentiles (10:1—28:31)
Peter's Activities (10:1—12:25)

In this narrative, Peter is confronted with his religiosity by God himself through a canvas with "unclean" animals (Acts 10:1—16).

God had to change Peter's mindset, because he had not understood that the Gospel was also for the Gentiles (whom he considered to be unclean).

Do we also have mental religious structures that prevent us from fulfilling the mission?

Print the canvas corresponding to this lesson at www.e625.com/lessons.

Make two teams to fill those canvases, answering the question: What does God want us to use that we've been unable to use in the past?

God worked in Peter's heart so that he would be willing to go to the house of Cornelius, a Gentile, and present the Gospel to him (10:34-44). We must decide to break with the structures that limit us from following our mission, and to embrace God's new paradigm.
(In the next lesson we will see the rest of the structure.)

Download at www.e625.com/lessons the complementary material for this section.

Important questions, important decisions

Are we willing to become "the continuation of the Gospels"? Are we willing to live the book of Acts?

What do we need in order to become "witnesses"? What things must we suffer, or could we suffer, for becoming witnesses?

What about Jesus?

Jesus is the Risen One, he who appears in the lives of many to transform them. Jesus is the one who sends us his Spirit and dwells in us to propel us to spread the Gospel to the ends of the earth.

Decide

Today I decide to become a witness of Jesus and his resurrection, wherever I may be, at home or far from it. I promise to attest to what God has done in the world and in my own life.

To pray is a good decision. Take time to pray before dismissal.

Remember to download the daily readings, For Depth and Applications, from www.e625.com/lessons.

Lesson 29 > ACTS 13—28

Paul, the missionary to the ends of the earth

The extension of the message of hope continues, this time in the hands of Paul of Tarsus, the persecutor of the church who met Jesus on the way to Damascus.

He will be sent by the church to which he belongs (Antioch) to share the Gospel throughout the empire, he will plant new churches in various cities, he will share the Gospel throughout present-day Turkey, he will also pass through Greece and end up in Rome. Three of his journeys are recorded in Acts (possibly there were more), and we will try to reconstruct together in this lesson his journeys and also his teachings.

Paul had to learn to depend on God's voice at all times to know what to do. We must also learn to listen to God's voice in the mission he has entrusted to us.

 Download at www.e625.com/lessons the complementary material for this section.

Division and structure

Paul's first missionary journey (13:1–14:28)
The council at Jerusalem (15:1—35)

This council occurred after Paul's first missionary trip, and in it the decision was made that Gentiles could become part of God's people, without the need to be circumcised or become part of the Jewish people. This was an extraordinary leap in the Christian mission to the world, and the result of this is that we are here today.

Paul's second missionary journey (15:36–18:22)

Paul's third missionary journey (18:23–20:38)
Paul's imprisonment and trip to Rome (21:1–28:31)

Finally Paul is arrested but he will continue to share the Gospel wherever he goes, before authorities, dignitaries and perhaps finally before Caesar himself. Thus what was said in Acts 9:15—16 was fulfilled. Do you remember it?

Divide into three groups that will be the missionary teams. Let's imagine that we travel with Paul to make a record of everything that happens, as mission correspondents. Each one of the groups will study one of Paul's trips by completing the data requested, and then in order they will present the information to the rest of the group.

Download the sheet with the first-century missionary report from www.e625.com/lessons, so your adolescents can complete it.

This is what Luke did: he collected what happened during that time and that is why it has come down to us today. We are extremely grateful to the brave people who decided to live the adventure of being guided by God to the ends of the earth!

Important questions, important decisions

What do we learn from Paul's missionary journeys?

Would we be willing to go wherever the Lord calls us? Why?

What things would be difficult for us to leave behind to follow our calling?

What about Jesus?

Jesus is the best news that we can give to the world, he is the one who presents the only true God in the midst of all the gods of Athens, he is that unknown God that we have been called to make known.

Decide

I decide to live the adventure of following Jesus wherever he leads me, and to be a faithful heir with those who in the book of Acts became witnesses of the resurrection.

 To pray is a good decision. Take time to pray before dismissal.

 Remember to download the daily readings, For Depth and Applications, from www.e625.com/lessons.

Lesson 30 > JAMES
Saved by faith, for works

We have now arrived at one of the most practical books in the New Testament, since it is like an instruction manual for the Christian life. Not everyone likes instruction manuals, but they are useful; many of us would be unable to assemble a piece of furniture without instructions, or we would assemble it incorrectly.

James is an eminently practical, rather than theological, letter. It deals with various topics in a condensed way: facing trials, doing rather than just hearing, being impartial, the use of language, and things that go beyond theoretical theological statements.

The central idea will be that faith without works is dead.

What does this last sentence mean?

We know that we are saved by grace (Ephesians 2:8) but there is no doubt that works go along with what we believe, and they are the natural demonstration of our faith. If the coal of faith is burning in the locomotive of our life, the wagons of works will move.

James will make us reflect on our deeds, our actions toward others, and on how we should act in a way that's consistent with what we believe.

The letter was written by James, probably a brother of Jesus, and a leader at one time in the church in Jerusalem.

We discover in James someone who is concerned that we become not only hearers of the Word but also doers (read James 1:22—25).

What is the difference between being a "doer" of the word and being only a "hearer"?

What is the consequence of being only a "hearer"?

The consequence is that we are fooling ourselves. Many adolescents go to church and take part in its activities, but in this text we are reminded that if we do not put the Word into practice, we are fooling ourselves, believing ourselves to be good Christians just because we hear the message, and attend church, when God is calling us to something more.

This book will remind us a bit of the books of wisdom from the Old Testament, such as Proverbs. We will see some practical advice that James wants us to remember and that will enable us to make good decisions in our Christian life.

In this lesson we will review the entire epistle, highlighting its important points. You may want to recommend that they use a physical Bible, so they don't lose the thread of the teaching.

Download at www.e625.com/lessons the complementary material for this section.

Division and structure

- Greeting (1:1)
- The wisdom that comes from God (1:2–11)
- Victory in trials (1:12–18)
- Doers of the word (1:19–27)

After inviting us to be doers, he tells us the following:

> Religion that God our Father accepts as pure and faultless is this: to look after orphans and widows in their distress and to keep oneself from being polluted by the world. (James 1:27)

Here we see that religion (in a positive sense, that is, following a way of life) has two important points: one active and one passive.

What are they?

On the one hand, the practical part of loving our neighbor (in this case, caring for those in need) and on the other, keeping ourselves clean from corruption. This would be a good summary of the Christian life.

Where are we most focused, in the active or the passive part?

Admonition against favoritism (2:1–13)
Faith without works (2:14–26)

Reading James 2:14—23, we can clearly see the point that works will go hand in hand with a sincere faith.

Lesson 30 > James

What practical decisions can we make by reading this text? Should we feel condemned, or should we act accordingly?

We must not believe only intellectually (demons believe and tremble) but our conduct, especially when it comes to loving our neighbor, must reflect our faith.

The tongue (3:1—12)

More excellent advice: [. . .] "For in many things we offend all." [. . .] (James 3:2 KJV)

Do you think this is true?

Help adolescents to see that we are not perfect, that we start from the truth that we all make bad decisions with what we say and do, and many times we hurt others. We always think that others hurt us, but what about us? Isn't it true that we hurt others?

God invites us to watch our language.

When do we tend to neglect our speech, or feel that we lose control over our tongue?

What practical things can we do to "bridle our tongue and our language"?

Make groups of two or three and have each group make a list of the things others say to us that bother us the most. It can be some curse words, or something said to hurt us, etc. Then share them with all the other groups, and respond by drawing conclusions. The idea is to learn not to say to others what we don't want them to say to us.

Wisdom from heaven (3:13—18)
Friendship with the world (4:1—10)

> Reading James 4:1—3 *we see that we should not blame our bad decisions on external influences. After all, we are the ones who decide what to do or not to do, and everything comes from our own passions, from within us. Let's take responsibility for our lives.*

Who are you to judge? (4:11—12)
Do not boast about tomorrow (4:13—17)
Against the rich oppressors (5:1—6)
Be patient and pray (5:7—20)

Read James 5:16. *This verse has often been taken out of context, so you have to remember that a text without context is just a pretext (especially the last part that says, "The prayer of a righteous person is powerful and effective").*

In which situations have we used this verse?
Let's read the first part and connect it with the second.

How do you think they are related?

This verse encourages us to help each other, to confess and accompany each other, as in this group. We are not here to judge or condemn each other, but to walk together in our walk with Jesus. It is in this context where effective prayer can be powerful.

Encourage the adolescents to pray for each other in pairs for a few minutes.

Important questions, important decisions

What do you think is the most important lesson in the epistle of James?

Of the things studied today, which one is the most difficult for you to put into practice?

What about Jesus?

Jesus is the Lord who comes not only to teach us wonderful ideas, but to bring us salvation and a new way of living, very practical and geared toward blessing our neighbors.

Decide

I decide to put into practice the teachings of Jesus, not to be a forgetful listener but instead a doer of the Word, in order to bless others.

To pray is a good decision. Take time to pray before dismissal.

Remember to download the daily readings, For Depth and Applications, from www.e625.com/lessons.

Lesson 31 > GALATIANS
Works don't save, only Jesus saves

On one of his missionary journeys, Paul founded a church in Galatia, which he later supervised and sometimes returned to visit. The Epistle to the Galatians is a letter addressed to a group of believers who started out very well and with great enthusiasm, but who had forgotten—influenced by false teachers—what the Gospel meant.

So around AD 50, Paul wrote this true Gospel manifesto to free the Galatians from unnecessary slavery.

That's what this letter is about: the Gospel is not just the first step to being a Christian, it's not just the ABC's, but rather it's the A to Z of the Christian life.

Galatians will give us a sense of freedom from religiosity. Many of us still think that to get salvation we have to do something, and we live as slaves, trying to fulfill the law. That was what happened to the Galatians, where a false teaching was introduced telling them that they needed to be circumcised, that Jesus was not enough.

How would you define the Gospel?

We will see that the problem is not just the Galatians' lack of obedience, but it is putting our trust in our own obedience, in our good works. This never brings anything good, only spiritual pride or guilt.

We must remember that it's all about the undeserved favor that God gave to us, and that God loves us just as we are—and not as we should be—and that the Gospel message is for every day. We must also remember that we are wicked, sinners, worse than we think. But we are loved more than we can ever comprehend, and we are accepted in Christ. This truth gives us freedom and it changes everything.

Let's delve into this letter so we don't forget that Jesus is enough for our salvation, and we should not be anybody's slaves.

What does it mean to you that God loves you just the way you are and not the way you should be?

Division and structure
We will see in this letter three main parts (without counting the prologue or the epilogue):

- Prologue (1:1—9)
- The Gospel announced by Paul (1:10—2:21)
- Faith and Christian freedom (3:1—5:12)
- The use of freedom (5:13—6:10)
- Epilogue (6:11—18)

The prologue tells us what the letter will be about:

> I am astonished that you are so quickly deserting the one who called you to live in the grace of Christ and are turning to a different Gospel—which is really no Gospel at all. Evidently some people are throwing you into confusion and are trying to pervert the Gospel of Christ. (Galatians 1:6—7)

Although they had received the Gospel of grace, they had soon switched to "a different" Gospel because there were people who were "throwing them into confusion." Paul wrote this letter to clarify things and to present Christ's message faithfully.

The Gospel announced by Paul (1:10—2:21)
In this first big section, Paul defends the authenticity of his message. He will tell his own story, that he was a Jew and persecuted the church, but was liberated to share the Gospel.

(Read Galatians 2:16—21 and study it carefully.)

In this manifesto we see the answers to some questions.

Who can be justified by the works of the law?

How can we be justified and forgiven?

Is this an excuse to do whatever we want?

God calls us to live by faith, trusting in him and in what he did.

Galatians 2:20 is a key verse for many.

What does this text mean to you?

Lesson 31 > Galatians

Faith and Christian freedom (3:1—5:12)

In the central part of the letter there is a warning to those who try to live in external religiosity, by trying to follow the Law. Paul gives as an example Abraham (the father of faith), and then he invites us to be firm:

> It is for freedom that Christ has set us free. Stand firm, then, and do not let yourselves be burdened again by a yoke of slavery. (Galatians 5:1)

God calls us to be free, not to keep up with external precepts and commandments.

What is religiosity?

Jesus has set us free from ritualisms that have no content. Today, many of us think of complying with external "Christian" things, thinking that this will bring us salvation, and we forget about the central message of the Gospel.

The use of freedom (5:13—6:10)

When we delve deeper into the message of the Gospel and become free, we must not use that freedom as an occasion to indulge the flesh (that part of us that wants to sin) but we must use our freedom to do what's good for others (read Galatians 5: 13—14).

According to Paul, how do we sum up the entire law?

Let's think for a moment: the entire law. . . is a lot! But when Jesus frees us, he enables us to fulfill the entire law through love for our neighbor, not to earn salvation but because God has already granted it to us.

> Thus we can live, but not in the acts of the flesh (a list of which Paul provides; read it in *Galatians 5:19—21*).

All of these are "the acts of the flesh." Rather than trying to figure out which one is worse than the others, we must learn to avoid all of them.

Then Paul invites us to enjoy the fruit of the Spirit, which we must exhibit, instead of any external rituals.

> *But the fruit of the Spirit is love, joy, peace, forbearance, kindness, goodness, faithfulness, gentleness and self—control. Against such things there is no law. (Galatians 5:22—23)*

How can we exhibit each of the aspects of the fruit of the Spirit?

Let's not use freedom as a pretext. Many of us, knowing that we are saved by grace, believe that this is a "license to sin."

Why do you think that doesn't make sense?

Galatians tells us not to do this alone. We need each other (6:2, 9, 10).

Epilogue (6:11—18)

Here, Paul says that the false teachers "compel" them, in this case to be circumcised. But many times there are false teachers who "compel" us to perform religious rituals without content. That is not the Gospel.

> Let us learn to enjoy the freedom to which Christ has called us and accept the blessing of the last verse (Galatians 6:18).

Download at www.e625.com/lessons the complementary material for this section.

Important questions, important decisions

Are we in danger of living again based on rules and precepts? Under the law rather than by the message of the Gospel?

How can we enjoy the freedom that Jesus gives us?

In what practical ways can we love our neighbors today?

What do you think is the most important teaching in the epistle to the Galatians?

What about Jesus?

Jesus is the one who frees us from the slavery of the Law and gives us freedom to love God and our neighbor.

Lesson 31 > Galatians

Decide

I decide to be free from the human effort to save myself. I recognize the work of Jesus in me and decide to live according to the freedom that I already have in him.

 To pray is a good decision. Take time to pray before dismissal.

 Remember to download the daily readings, For Depth and Applications, from www.e625.com/lessons.

Lesson 32 > 1 AND 2 THESSALONIANS

The letters expecting the return of the King

Some say that Thessalonians is the New Testament book that was written first. Thessalonica was the capital of Macedonia, and Paul shared the Gospel with them. Apparently, a community of believers emerged and flourished, and it was to them that he dedicated these two letters. He was only there for about three weeks, but there was a riot and he had to flee. Shortly after establishing the church there he sent one of his associates, Timothy, to take them the first letter and strengthen the brethren in faith. Within a few months he sent a second epistle.

In these letters we see Paul's interest in educating the new believers who had questions, because Paul's letters are answers to questions that churches have.

This is an important principle in understanding Paul's epistles: they are responses to concrete things that were happening. Therefore, to do a good exegesis, we must understand the questions to which he was responding; otherwise, we can be completely wrong in our interpretation. Again, the context is important. A text without context is just a pretext.

- What should we do to cope with the persecution that we face?

- How should we behave as Christians?

- When will Jesus arrive, and what will happen to Christians who die before he returns?

These letters are the answer to those questions. The second one will have a more severe tone, since some exalted people thought that Christ had already returned and were creating problems for the congregation from within, even encouraging them not to work because Christ would be arriving soon.

If there had been telephones at that time, these letters would not have come to us. Paul had to practice discipleship from long distance, and the letters to the Thessalonians are the result.

Do you think this happens today? Why?

Lesson 32 > 1 and 2 Thessalonians

Division and structure

1 Thessalonians
- Prologue (1:1—10)
- Paul's ministry in Thessalonica (2:1—3:13)
- Exhortations (4:1—5:24)
- Epilogue (5:25—28)

2 Thessalonians
- Prologue (1:1—12)
- Instructions (2:1—3:15)
- The man of lawlessness (2:1—12)
- Chosen for salvation (2:13—17)
- May the word of God be glorified (3:1—5)
- The duty to work (3:6—15)
- Epilogue (3:16—18)

In this lesson we are going to do a study answering the three questions that began this study.

 Form three groups, and distribute the texts that deal with the subject to see Paul's answers; then we will share them with the others, so we can understand together the message to the Thessalonians.

 Download at www.e625.com/lessons the complementary material for this section.

 Your job in this session will be to supervise the three groups, to encourage them to draw practical conclusions and advice, and to clarify the meaning of the text. You can help them by repeating the question. Have them make a list gathering four or five important concepts, which they can then present to the whole group.

> **GROUP 1:** What should we do in order to cope with the persecution that we face?
> A case of bullying -
> Texts: 1 Thes. 3:4—8, 11—13 / 2 Thes. 1:3—12 / 2 Thes. 3:1—3

 The idea is to focus on the fact that persecution (bullying) due to being a Christian is something that we all go through in one way or another, even going so far as to give our lives. We must learn to stand firm and support each other, and make sure that our identity is well defined by what Jesus has done, and that social pressure does not discourage us nor does it make us give in.

GROUP 2: How should we behave as Christians?
Texts: 1 Thes. 1:6—10 / 1 Thes. 4:1—12 / 1 Thes. 5:14—24 / 2 Thes. 2:13—15 / 1 Thes. 3:11—15

There is a lot of good advice here (remind them that it was geared toward new believers). Pick up the ideas that attract their attention the most, and see how Paul was very practical, helping the Thessalonians make the best decisions as they took their first steps.

GROUP 3: When will Jesus arrive, and what will happen to Christians who die before he returns?
Texts: 1 Thes. 4:13—5:11 / 2 Thes. 2:1—12

Here we must avoid "evangelical sensationalism." Many want to know the day and the hour, but not even Jesus knew! The main thing is to hope for his return, and this should change our perspective on life. It is normal for us to be curious, and Paul gives us some information that is not exhaustive but is true.

Having this vision of the future helps us in making our decisions.

If Christ is to return, how should we behave?

If Christ is to return, we have hope when facing trials, because the story ends well.

Download at www.e625.com/lessons the complementary material for this section.

We see that these three questions that Paul answers in his letters are connected. The return of Jesus gives us hope in the midst of trials, and also indicates to us the way in which we should live, a life worthy of the King who will return soon. Let's be wise in our decisions and learn to stand firm until he returns.

Important questions, important decisions

What is the most important thing you have learned from these two epistles?

Why is it important to understand that Jesus is coming back?

Which piece of advice did you like the most?

What decisions did these letters from Paul prompt you to make?

Lesson 32 > 1 and 2 Thessalonians

What about Jesus?

Jesus is the one who will return, and who gives meaning to our present. We also live with our eyes on the future, in the hope that what we do now will be rewarded and we will stand firm.

Decide

I decide to stand firm in the teachings of Jesus, trusting that he will return, and learning to share my faith without fear of rejection or lack of understanding.

 To pray is a good decision. Take time to pray before dismissal.

 Remember to download the daily readings, For Depth and Applications, from www.e625.com/lessons.

Lesson 33 > 1ST CORINTHIANS
A troubled church

Corinth was probably the most contentious church you could ever imagine.

Imagine the worst church you can think of. What conflicts would it have? What terrible problems would it have?

The idea is to visualize the situation in Corinth. In this lesson we will discover a very troubled church, and the way that Paul approaches it. We will focus on the concept of love over gifts, and how we should make our decisions based on loving others rather than being partisan, playing favorites, or being lax with sin.

The only solution for our lives is the mutual understanding and forgiveness that Jesus offers us. In this lesson we will see the chapter on love and how our gifts have to be exercised by loving others. We must make our decisions based on love to overcome all problems, no matter how difficult circumstances are.

Division and structure

- Prologue (1:1—9)
- Divisions in the church (1:10—4:21)
- Paul corrects the church (5:1—6:20)
- On marriage (7:1—40)
- Christian freedom (8:1—11:1)
- The life of the church (11:2—34)
- The gifts of the Holy Spirit (12:1—14:40)
- The resurrection of the dead (15:1—58)
- Epilogue (16:1—24)

Prologue (1:1—9)
Let's read verse 2: *"To the church of God in Corinth, to those sanctified in Christ Jesus and called to be his holy people, together with all those everywhere who call on the name of our Lord Jesus Christ—their Lord and ours."*

What does it mean for them to be "sanctified" and "called to be his holy people"?

Even though the Corinthians were already saved ("sanctified"), we will see that God calls them to be holy. They were still in the process. In the epistle we will see that they were very far from perfect. . . and it is to them that this letter is addressed.

Divisions in the church (1:10—4:21)
(Read 1 Corinthians 1:10—13.)

What was one of the problems that they had in Corinth?

Why did they have it?

There are many schools of thought, but we cannot allow divisions based on claims of belonging to Apollos or to Pau. We are called to return to Jesus, and realize thathe is the protagonist.

It all centers on him and on what he did for us (1 Corinthians 2:2).

What are the dangers of being a partisan?

Paul corrects the church (5:1—6:20)
After talking about the importance of unity and of not speaking ill of others, Paul corrects the church.

According to 1 Corinthians 5:9—11, what was another of the problems of the church?

Do you think that it matters who we hang out with? To what extent can it harm us or benefit us?

An important point that you can deal with in this section is the importance in making decisions and choosing the people with whom we get together and spend time.

An important verse that many of us know is 1 Corinthians 6:12 (read it).

Have you ever thought about what it means?

Although everything is legal, it does not mean that everything is beneficial. It is important to see that when we make decisions, making a bad decision is not necessarily doing something that is obviously a sin. Sometimes we have to learn to discern between what is good, what is permitted, and what is best.

On marriage (7:1—40)
Christian freedom (8:1—11:1)

Many times we argue over our various opinions on different topics. We love being right. We may have different thoughts on many issues, but that's no reason to look down on each other. As Saint Augustine said:

> "In essentials, unity; in doubtful matters, liberty; in all things, charity."

Respecting others and not judging them is part of the Christian's life, but the Corinthians apparently did not fully understand this.

> We know that "We all possess knowledge." But knowledge puffs up while love builds up. (1 Corinthians 8:1)

What does this sentence mean (see 8:9—13)?

If what we know does not help our brother but causes him to stumble, we are doing it wrong.

In this section we also see that the Corinthians had problems with idolatry. What a church! But there is more.

The life of the church (11:2—34)
(Read 1 Corinthians 11:17—22.)

What new problem is added?

They abused the Lord's Supper. Something that should be done in memory of Jesus' love for us and to celebrate communion had also become an excuse for more divisiveness.

The gifts of the Holy Spirit (12:1—14:40)

Paul talks about the gifts of the Holy Spirit, and encourages us to have unity in the midst of diversity.

(Read 1 Corinthians 12:4—7.)

And the gifts that we have are meant to benefit all.

Do you know what gifts you have?

Lesson 33 > 1st Corinthians

Your gifts are for the benefit of others, to love them, and love is the focus of 1 Corinthians 13.

Let's read it together.
Love is the greatest thing we have and it should be the engine of our lives, our actions and our decisions. It is not a feeling nor is it something temporary. It is much deeper and we must put it into practice, not just have it as a pretty word.

Download the sheet "I am a gift to others" from www.e625.com/lessons.

On this card, each teen puts his name in the blank space. Sitting in a circle, he passes the card to the person to his right, who responds to the question, "What gifts does _____ (the person whose name is written) have that bless my life?" He talks for one or two minutes. Then he passes it on to the person to his right, who answers the same question about him, and so on.

Each adolescent has a card that he will pass to his right while he answers the question about the person whose name is on the card that comes from his left. In this way, at the end of the activity, they will receive her file with what everyone in the group has written.

If the group is very large, divide them into groups of no more than eight or nine people.

They should only put positive things like his smile, he know how to listen, he understands me, he is a friend, he helps me, he has the gift of speaking well, he inspires me.

The resurrection of the dead (15:1—58)
At the end of the letter we find one of the oldest statements of faith that exist, and it summarizes the message of the Gospel.

(Read 1 Corinthians 15:3—7.)

It's a summary of the story of Jesus and the resurrection. That message remains transformative today.

In chapter 15 he talks about the resurrection and how it affects us. It is important to remember the end of our story, to be able to make good decisions in our present.

Epilogue (16:1—24)
Let's read 1 Corinthians 16:13, and the last verse (16:24).

What was Paul biggest concern about the Corinthians?

Download at www.e625.com/lessons the complementary material for this section.

Important questions, important decisions

What do we learn from this letter about what is most important?

What has caught your attention the most about the church in Corinth?

What about Jesus?

Jesus is love incarnate, and put into practice at its utmost expression. He is our unity and our message.

Decide

I decide that love will be the foundation of my actions and decisions.

To pray is a good decision. Take time to pray before dismissal.

Remember to download the daily readings, For Depth and Applications, from www.e625.com/lessons.

Lesson 34 > 2ND CORINTHIANS

But the story of Corinth does not end here. This second letter (or third, since there may be another one that was lost) tells us that the problems were not completely solved, and new ones appeared. Reality is sometimes harsher than we may think, and the environment at the city of Corinth did not help the believers. n fact, there was a libertine way of acting that at that time was called "do it as Corinthians"; "live as the Corinthians" (in Greek, *korinthiazomai*). I hope they don't say these things about the city where we live.

This will be Paul's most autobiographical letter and the most difficult for him to write.

Trying to confuse God's people, false teachers arose who spoke ill of Paul and promoted Judaizing teachings, as was the case in Galatia.

What would be the hardest thing for you to forgive?

How do you act or react when you find out that someone speaks ill of you?

What is the best decision in these cases?

Division and structure

The epistle is divided into three large sections, in which we will see a sincere Paul defending his ministry from the attacks he received.

Download the structure sheet of 2 Corinthians from www.e625.com/lessons

Divide the teens into two or three working groups to explore the first section of the letter. We answer the questions in teams and then present the answers to the other groups, so that they fill in the sections that they have not worked on, to complete the work.

You must facilitate the work of the groups, approaching them and asking them what they need or where they are. Encourage them to continue with the study and give them clues, but not answers. This dynamic should consist of a maximum of twenty minutes of preparation, and then the presentation to the other groups.

When they do the presentation, have them defend their answers with verses from the text. In the guide you can see the texts. Read those texts with them.

Prologue (1:1—11)

Paul speaks here of troubles and comfort. Although we will see that it is a letter in which he is going to correct the Corinthians, that does not mean that he puts himself above them. He shares in their struggles, so that they can comfort each other (1:5—7).

Paul defends his ministry and brings comfort (1:12—7:16)
- Paul's conduct (1:12—2:11)

What is Paul's attitude in this section?

It is an attitude of forgiveness, understanding, and humility (1:12, 24; 2:1, 4, 5).

How did he encourage the Corinthians to treat the person who has offended them?

With love and forgiveness, not with condemnation (2:5—11).

When you present this section, stress the importance that, no matter how offended we feel, we should always have an attitude of forgiveness. Forgiveness is always a good decision.

Characteristic of Paul's ministry (2:12—6:10)

What is the title he holds, or the letter of recommendation that Pablo presents?

The letter is not a title, but the Corinthians themselves are his own work. He does not base his authority on the title but on his love for them (3:1—6).

With what attitude does Paul, being an apostle, approach the Corinthians in chapter 4?

He does not preach about himself, but comes as their servant for Jesus' sake (read 2 Corinthians 4:5—7).

What is the ministry that Paul has, according to chapter 5? Preaching? Healing? What does it consist of?

Here we will find one of the most incredible verses from Scripture (5:19) and his response (5:20): the ministry of reconciliation. Given the situation that the church in Corinth finds itself in, this verse takes on even more force, doesn't it?

Lesson 34 > 2nd Corinthians

Call to the Corinthians (6:11—7:4)

What does he ask the Corinthians to do?

To act with integrity (6:13), to not be unequally yoked (6:14), and to purify themselves from all contamination, seeking holiness (7:1).

The comfort of the ministry (7:5—16)

Paul here reaffirms the Corinthians with love.

What do we learn from this whole section?

As much as some may have hurt us or talked against us, we must approach them with love, keeping in mind that we are called to reconciliation.

Review the following two sections based on the time you have had in the previous dynamic. We recommend that you set aside at least ten minutes to go over some of the context and the application.

The offering for the saints in Jerusalem (8:1—9:15)

Throughout this section, Paul calls for solidarity from the Christians in Corinth toward the Christians in Jerusalem who are in need. Apparently, at first they were willing to help, but at the time of the offering they were not as inclined, so Paul had to write this section.

This issue of the offering for the brothers in Jerusalem will be seen in other epistles of Paul. He wanted the churches of the Diaspora (those outside of Israel) to give offerings to the needy in Jerusalem (see Romans 15:26).

- Plans for the offering (8:1—24)
- Arguments for the offering (9:1—15)

In this section, Paul appears more serious and defends his ministry from the attacks he has received. But he stresses that what is important is not his position as an apostle but his service to Jesus Christ.

Paul's new defense (10:1—13:10)
- Paul's position (10:1—12:18)
Let's read 2 Corinthians 10:17.

What advice does Paul give us here? Why do you think he says this? What do you think is happening in Corinth?

Do you think this happens to us? How?

- Paul's purpose (12:19—13:10)

Epilogue (13:11—14)

Here we see a perfect summary of what Paul wanted to accomplish with this letter (we can read it in full before concluding the lesson).

Important questions, important decisions

What do you think was the main purpose of 2 Corinthians?

Do you think Paul made a good decision in writing this letter? Why?

Do you think he acted wisely? Why?

What about Jesus?

In Jesus, God is reconciling the world to himself (5:19). We must have that same attitude, not taking into account the sins and insults of others. Forgiving is always a good decision, and Jesus taught us to do that.

Decide

I decide to forgive as Jesus forgave me, always seeing in the needs and mistakes of my neighbor not an opportunity to judge but a chance to serve.

To pray is a good decision. Take time to pray before dismissal.

Remember to download the daily readings, For Depth and Applications, from www.e625.com/lesosns.

Lesson 35 > ROMANS (PART 1)
The just shall live by faith (part 1)

Paul had not visited the church in Rome, and because of that we have the letter to the Romans as it is. The closest thing to a presentation of the Gospel, of God's plan, in a systematic and clear way, using above all the legal metaphor. Many of the changes that occurred during the history of the church (and of the world) have happened thanks to the rediscovery of this letter. Martin Luther deepened the idea that Romans develops: "The just shall live by faith," based on the verse from the prophet Habakkuk. This brought what is now known as the Reformation, a movement that forever changed the church, as well as the map of Europe and the world.

In Romans we find well-known verses that help us to remember what the Gospel is.

Can you say in your own words what the Gospel is?

In these two lessons we are going to take a bird's-eye view of Romans, studying its structure in depth to see how Paul teaches us what the Gospel is and how to make our decisions in light of it (starting with Romans 12). We will analyze together the content and the main verses of this text. Perhaps it will revolutionize our lives as it has so many others.

To accomplish this, we will make two teams. In the first section of Romans, the two teams will represent the first and the second parts of the text (God's wrath and God's grace), and in the second section the two teams will represent the third and fourth sections (God's plan and God's will).

The four sections correspond to the four themes of Romans: God's wrath, God's grace, God's plan, and God's will. In the end, we will have a complete picture of the message of Romans.

Download at www.e625.com/lessons the complementary material for this section.

First we'll do the group dynamics and then we'll review the text.

Complete the first two sections.

1- God's wrath (1:18—3:20)

For the assigned team to complete the task: What are the problems humans have, according to this section? (Use these verses as a guide to answer: 1:21—24 / 1:29—32 / 2:1, 5, 21—24 / 3:10—12.)

Download the Romans diagram from www.e625.com/lessons.

2- God's grace (3:21—8:39)

For the assigned team to complete the task: How does God solve the problems that humans have? How does he act within us?

(Use these verses as a guide to answer: 3:23—25 / 5:1—2, 6, 10.)

Division and structure

Prologue (1:1—17)

Here we find Paul's intention in writing to the Romans, the main idea that Paul is going to present (read Romans 1: 16—17).

> *"The righteous will live by faith."*

This will be the idea that Paul is going to build on. As a present—day preacher, he will take that verse from the prophet Habakkuk (Habakkuk 2:4) and develop it throughout the epistle.

What do you think this verse means?

Paul explains the Gospel to us in a clear manner. Looking at the structure of Romans, we will discover what Paul means by Gospel: the good news. We will see how God makes the unjust become just in a way that is just.

1. God's wrath (1:18—3:20)

Wait a moment! If this is good news, why does it start with the wrath of God?
The Gospel tells us about our real situation. We cannot give good news to someone who is sick by telling him that there is a cure if we do not first make a good diagnosis of the disease. That is what Paul is doing throughout the first three chapters.

Before studying the book of Romans, what do you think Romans will state is the problem humans have? The diagnosis? The solution to the problem?

Lesson 35 > Romans (Part 1)

Go over what the "God's wrath" group has worked on, and the dynamics they have exposed.

2. God's grace (3:21—8:39)

This section presents the solution. In verse 21 Paul says "but now" and it is one of the greatest game changers in the Bible.

How would you describe the grace of God?

Romans 3:23—25 is one of the texts that best sums up what God has done to change our condition. This was one of Martin Luther's favorite texts.

For chapter 4:

Why is Abraham's example important?

Abraham was justified by faith, by trusting in God.

For chapter 6:

Is God's grace the perfect excuse to sin (read Romans 6:1—6)?

Here we should point out that grace is not an excuse, but it is what helps us to make better decisions, to receive God's forgiveness and to be able to serve him.

For chapter 7:

Spiritual schizophrenia is wanting to do two contradictory things at once (read Romans 7:15—25).

Can you identify with this text? Why?

What can we do to make good decisions in the midst of this "schizophrenia"?

Thank God that after chapter 7 comes chapter 8. What a relief!

For chapter 8:

What is our hope? (Romans 8:28—39)

This passage is an expression of praise for God's unconditional love. Based on this assurance, let's learn to be led by the Spirit.

The whole BIBLE in a year for HIGH SCHOOL

How can we be led by the Spirit?
Let's read some verses from the first part of Romans 8.

How do we apply this to our decision making?

Important questions, important decisions

Do you think the Gospel as presented in Romans makes sense? Why?

Do you think there is another way for us to be saved? Why?

What about Jesus?

Jesus is the one who makes the unjust become just in a way that is just. He is our justice, our hope.

Decide

I decide to live and experience the power of the Gospel that justifies me and transforms me, and to delve into what it means that "the just shall live by faith."

To pray is a good decision. Take time to pray before dismissal.

Remember to download the daily readings, For Depth and Applications, from www.e625.com/lessons

Lesson 36 > ROMANS (PART 2)

Continuing with the dynamics of the previous lesson, we will make two teams to cover the two sections that we still have to study. Have the teens answer the suggested questions and then make a three to four minutes presentation to the other team.

Download at www.e625.com/lessons the complementary material for this section.

3- God's plan (9:1—11:36)
For the assigned team to complete the task:

What happened to the people of Israel? How does that point to Jesus? Did God want to save Gentiles in the Old Testament? (Use these verses as a guide to answer: 9:4, 5 / 9:10—13 / 9:24—26 / 11:11—12.)

4- God's will (12:1—15:13)
For the assigned team to complete the task:

If God has done everything that we are told in Romans 1 through 11, how should we act now?

(Use these verses as a guide to answer: 12:1—3 / 12:9—21 / 13:1.)

Division and structure

God's plan (9:1—11:36)
This is a very complex section, in which we find difficult texts, such as Romans 9:13 (read the text).

What do you think of this verse?

But this is also a wonderful text, because we see that Jesus is not an improvisation from God but, from the time of Abraham, Isaac and Jacob, he already was working his plan of salvation for all (including the Gentiles). He allowed all of Old Testament history to lead to the person of Jesus (because God does not improvise). The entire Bible—as we have seen in all of these lessons—points to Jesus.
God plans history. We also need to plan in order to make good decisions.

Do you think that God has everything planned and that we are not free? Were the decisions that we make already in God's mind? How does this affect our decisions today?

This is a recurring theme in many teenage conversations. The idea is not to discuss the subject in a negative way, but to expose the mystery that it entails. We must learn to trust God's plan while taking responsibility for our own free actions.

God's will (12:1—15:13)

This is the most practical section, and this is how it begins (read Romans 12:1—2).

> *If everything said from chapter 1 through chapter 11 (see the outline of the entire book) is true, and God has justified us, our natural response, our spiritual worship, and our logical reaction is to offer our life for him, to decide to give ourselves entirely to him.*

But giving ourselves to him implies living for others. From 12:4 to the end of this section, the theme that puts everything into focus is how we should treat others, because giving ourselves to God is loving our neighbor.

Do you think it is possible to love and give ourselves to God for what he has done and not live our lives loving others? Why?

Epilogue (15:14—16:27)

In this last section Paul talks about his ministry, and says that he wants to preach the Gospel where it has not yet been preached (v. 20). He tells them that he wants to visit Rome and sends personal greetings.

The final farewell is a good summary of all that he wrote.

> *Now to him who is able to establish you in accordance with my Gospel, the message I proclaim about Jesus Christ, in keeping with the revelation of the mystery hidden for long ages past, but now revealed and made known through the prophetic writings by the command of the eternal God, so that all the Gentiles might come to the obedience that comes from faith—to the only wise God be glory forever through Jesus Christ! Amen. (Romans 16:25—27)*

God's plan of salvation, which has always been a mystery for many centuries, designed to save humanity, is the Gospel of Jesus! That is why we praise him and serve him!

Lesson 36 > Romans (Part 2)

Important questions, important decisions

What has caught your attention the most about the epistle to the Romans? How does what Jesus has done for us affect my life in practical terms?

Is there anything that you think you should do, now that you know that the Gospel has justified you?

What about Jesus?

Jesus is the one who saves us. We must confess thathe is Lord, and believe in our hearts that God raised him from the dead, and he encourages us to live a life of service to others as proof of our being justified.

Decide

I decide to experience God's grace in order to share that grace with others, especially with my family and my fellow believers.

 To pray is a good decision. Take time to pray before dismissal.

 Remember to download the daily readings, For Depth and Applications, from www.e625.com/lessons.

Lesson 37 > EPHESIANS

Living being the church

Ephesus was an important city in Asia. With some 300,000 inhabitants, it was one of the largest cities in the Roman Empire. Paul often passed through Ephesus; on one occasion he stayed for almost three years and established a church there.

Download at www.e625.com/lessons the complementary material for this section.

This letter, along with Romans, is one of the most systematic and educational for everyone, and deals with great theological themes that apply in a general way but from a different perspective. The first part is theoretical and will lay the foundation, just like the first part of Romans (chapters 1—11). The second part will focus on the life of the church. It is more practical, and talks about what a community of followers of Jesus is, and how it should function. Only by living this way can we be like him. Paul will finish by encouraging us to put on the full armor of God. We should not forget that we are in a battle, not against people but against something much more dangerous.

In this lesson, the emphasis will be that it is not enough to "have a personal relationship with God." He has placed us in a local church, the natural habitat for us to grow. Let's talk in this session about the importance of coming together, getting to know each other, helping one another, and speaking the truth with love. In short, loving our neighbor is a fundamental part of christianity.

What is more important: having a personal relationship with God, or having a relationship with God together as a church?

Describe the structure of Ephesians from a bird's-eye view, mentioning the parts. Ask the group the comprehension questions as they go through its structure, and encourage them to search the text for the answers. You can choose to do them all or pick the ones you consider most important for the teenagers. Remember that one of the objectives of these lessons is for them to see each book or letter of the Bible as a whole, with meaning, not just as individual verses.

Lesson 37 > Ephesians

Division and structure

Foundation (Theorical Part)
Prologue (1:1—2)

- God's saving work (1:3—3:21)
- God's choice (1:3—12)
- The seal of the Spirit (1:13—23)
- Salvation by grace through faith (2:1—10)
- Unity of the body of Christ (2:11—22)
- Mystery of the body of Christ (3:1—21)

Praxis (Practical Part)
Christian life (4:1—6:20)

- Worthy walk (4:1—6)
- Build up the body with the gifts (4:7—16)
- Put on the new man (4:17—32)
- Be imitators of God (5:1—21)
- Promote family harmony (5:22—6:9)
- The armor of God (6:10—20)
- Final greetings (6:21—24)

Foundation (Theorical Part)
Prologue (1:1—2)

- God's saving work (1:3—3:21)
- God's choice (1:3—12)

❓ Why did God choose us (1:4—7)?

— The seal of the Spirit (1:13—23)

❓ What spirit does the Lord give us? What for (1:17)?

— Salvation by grace through faith (2:1—10)

❓ How do grace, faith, and works work together (2:8—10)?

Remind them: we are not saved BY works but FOR good works.

Unity of the body of Christ (2:11—22)

Mystery of the body of Christ (3:1—21)

PRAXIS (PRACTICAL PART)

The Christian life (4:1—6:20)
- Worthy walk (4:1—6)
- Build up the body with the gifts (4:7—16)
- Put on the new man (4:17—32)

How do people walk without God (vv. 17—19)?

How do we put on the new man in a practical way (vv. 22—32)?

How does it affect our decisions?

Be imitators of God (5:1—21)
In this section we are encouraged to make decisions as God would make them.

Why do you think this is important?

If you have time, review the practical advice presented in the text and encourage teenagers to live it.

Promote family harmony (5:22—6:9)
    Read Ephesians 6:1—2.

What do you honestly think of these verses?

The armor of God (6:10—20)

Read the text in groups of two people. Which part of the armor do you think is the most important? Why? If you had to choose three, which ones would you keep?

Final greetings (6:21—24)
Let's live Ephesians 4

Lesson 37 > Ephesians

What would an ideal church modeled on Ephesians 4 look like to you? Have the teens form groups of three or four people to discuss the question and come up with an answer. Then each group will present to everyone our ideal church, based on the biblical texts.

Download Ephesians lesson sheet 2 from www.e625.com/lessons and have them read the passage from Ephesians 4:1—16 to complete the activity. Have them answer the questions below the text

Important questions, important decisions

What has caught your attention the most in the letter to the Ephesians?

How can I get involved in the spiritual life of others?

How is my commitment to my local church? What can I improve?

What about Jesus?

Ephesians reminds us that we are in Christ and that we have been created in Christ. Jesus is our reason for being and our goal.

Decide

I decide to live in community in order to grow and be like Jesus.

To pray is a good decision. Take time to pray before dismissal.

Remember to download the daily readings, For Depth and Applications, from www.e625.com/lessons.

Lesson 38 > PHILIPPIANS

Joy (from a prison)

This is one of Paul's most intimate letters. He writes it from prison with endearing love for a community that he holds in high esteem, and constantly encourages them to have joy regardless of the circumstances. We will find in it a song that the first Christians sang (Paul often included songs in his epistles) to remind them what their attitude should be, based on the decisions that Jesus himself made. What better example to follow in our decisions than Christ himself?

In this letter Paul engages in a very paternal, reflective and calm tone. It is a letter of thanksgiving, in which he will encourage the Philippians to move forward toward the goal, as athletes do during the Olympic games (Philippians 3:13—14).

How would you feel if you were a prisoner in jail?

Have you ever felt trapped in a situation without a solution or an answer? How do you think joy can be had at that moment?

Division and structure

Briefly explain the structure and focus on the themes and sections that we plan to develop, especially in the central part of the letter.

- Greeting (1:1—2)
- Paul's prayer for the Philippians (1:3—11)
- Paul's biography (1:12—26)
- The central part of the letter (1:27—4:9)
- Blessings and thanksgiving (4:10—23)

Let's read Philippians 2:1—4.

What are bad reasons to make decisions? What are good reasons?

  - *Bad: contention, vanity, selfishness*
  - *Good: humility, valuing others above ourselves, looking out for the interests of others*

Lesson 38 > Philippians

What does "valuing others above ourselves" mean?

(Read Philippians 1:17—18.)

Paul is in a difficult situation: he in prison.

What is his attitude in spite of that? Why do you think it is so?

Examples: Timothy, Epaphroditus (2:19—30)
Example of promise: 3:1—21

(Read Philippians 3:4—8.)

What is Paul's priority?

Christ. Knowing him.

It's not that all other things are bad, but that in comparison to knowing Jesus, everything else is rubbish. Often in our lives we have other priorities—even good ones—,but we must not forget that nothing is comparable to knowing Jesus.

(Read Philippians 3:13—14.)

The spiritual life is a race. Paul had not finished it yet, and likewise we also keep running. We must leave behind the wrong decisions, the priorities that don't belong where we have them, and move toward Jesus. Always.

As we get to the excellent promise (4:1—9), mention Philippians 4:4.

Considering Paul's situation, what he says becomes even more meaningful.

Have you ever felt distressed?

Look at what Philippians 4:6—7 says.

How can we have peace in the midst of any circumstance?

Have you ever experienced peace in a difficult situation? Would you like to share it?

Perhaps you can briefly share a personal experience to break the ice.

Blessings and thanksgiving (4:10—23)

Download Philippians 2 from www.e625.com/lessons.

Read the text in groups of three or four people. This text tells us about the attitude of Jesus, how he did not seek his own interests but the interests of others. Have them study the text and answer the following questions.

What is it that strikes you the most about Jesus' attitude?

How can you apply this to your decisions?

What is the end result?

To finish, still in groups, have them compose in their own words a poem, a rap or a text based on this song. They can use similar words or creative ideas that mark how Jesus humbled himself and how he ends up being exalted as the Lord. As an example, you can listen to this song inspired by Philippians 2:

Download at www.e625.com/lessons the complementary material for this section.

Important questions, important decisions

What has caught your attention the most in this text?

Do you think it is possible to always be joyful? Why?

This is a lesson in which we can focus on prayer, following Philippians 4:6—7. You can have the teens express a concern, in which they need the joy of the Lord. Remember that we are not here to teach a book, but to make disciples of adolescents who have needs and concerns, and in this generation they need above all the joy of Jesus.

What about Jesus?

Jesus is the example of true humility. He is incomparable, and striving to be like him is our goal.

Lesson 38 > Philippians

Decide

I decide to rejoice in the Lord always, following Paul's example—even in the midst of trouble—because I have the greatest joy anyone can ever experience: Jesus and the power of the resurrection.

 To pray is a good decision. Take time to pray before dismissal.

 Remember to download the daily readings, For Depth and Applications, from www.e625.com/lessons.

Lesson 39 > COLOSSIANS
How to become a "colossal" Christian

Let's remember that many of Paul's letters are in answer to specific situations being experienced by the churches to which they are addressed.

The problem is that we don't know what was happening in that community. We only know the answers that Paul gives, but not the questions. It is like listening to a telephone conversation but only hearing what the person next to us is saying. So we must infer the questions based on the answers. This happens in the epistle to the Colossians. We will do an exercise that will help us interpret this letter, and also the others.

"Next to the phone"
Form three groups with the teenagers. Present these answers, and infer the questions that were asked to get those answers. Then compare the answers of the different groups.

Encourage responses that are creative and funny but also make sense.

What are questions or phrases that may have generated these answers?
- "I won't be able to arrive on time, I'm sorry. Besides, I didn't buy the cake, but in any case Sophia should have bought it."
- "I am not to blame for what happened! Robert's car is 17 years old and it's a clunker".
- "You shouldn't believe what that one has taught you. Besides, the Bible says just the opposite: 'Love your neighbor as yourself'".
- "You should spend less money on those things and invest in what we talked about last week. Why did you change your mind so quickly?"

What conclusions can we draw from this exercise? Do you see why it's important to infer the questions that Paul was answering, and how it will help us understand better the content of the letters?

Colossae was a city in Phrygia, a province in Asia Minor. Some false doctrines had been introduced into the church at Colossae. On the one hand, there were the Judaizers, religious people who placed burdens on the Christians (a type of moralism that has always attacked the church throughout its history).

On the other hand, a type of primitive Gnosticism was being introduced, a mystical spirituality brought by people who believed themselves to be "enlightened," wiser than others, who generated spiritual pride (the worst type of pride) with strange ideas like the worship of angels and similar themes. Paul will remind them of who Jesus is and how he works in us, and he will encourage them to ignore both the mysticism and the legalism. He will focus instead on teaching them how to live a Christian life, beyond the rituals and ceremonies, a practical life in which Jesus is the center.

As in other letters of Paul, the first part is intended to establish a theological basis ("what God has done"), and then the second part leads us to answer: "So what should we do?" God's saving work, what Christ has done in us, precedes how we should act; that is Christianity. We cannot reverse the order, because it would not be Christianity but moralism (being good to be accepted). The Gospel is the opposite: we are accepted, therefore we can be good.

Division and structure

- Prologue (1:1—8)
- God's saving work (1:9—23)
- Paul's ministry (1:24—2:5)
- The new life in Christ (2:6—4:6)
- Epilogue (4:7—18)

  The problems of Colossae

 This exercise is similar to the one with the telephone that we did at the beginning, but this time it's based on the text of Colossians. Adolescents must complete their worksheet, for which we give you the corresponding answers to understand the context.

Download worksheet 1 from www.e625.com/lessons.

What is the problem to which Paul responds in each of these texts?

2:16—17 / 2:11 / 3:11
Ritualism, circumcision, legalism, permitted foods, religious festivities. . .

2:18
Worship of angels, superstition

2:21 / 2:23
Asceticism ("Don't touch. . .")

1:15—20 / 2:2—3, 9
Contempt for Christ (that is why emphasis is placed on his supremacy)

2:18 / 2:2—3
Occult sciences, gnosticism

We see that the church is stalked by many dangers, false doctrines and practices that we must be wary of, as they distract us from what is important: what God has done and how he works in us today.

What things distract us today from what is important in our theory and practice of the Christian life?

One of the characteristics of Paul's writings is the lists that he puts in many of his letters (good and bad things, gifts and sins, fruit of the Spirit, etc.). In Colossians we have an example of these lists, in the practical section of the text.

(Read Colossians 3:5—15.)

Download "in God's fashion" (tab 2) from www.e625.com/lessons.

Form two or three groups, read the text, and make two lists. What things should we get rid of? What things should we wear? How do we clothe ourselves in Christ? Then share the lists with the whole group.

How do these lists affect our decisions?

Download at www.e625.com/lessons the complementary material for this section.

Important questions, important decisions

What has caught your attention the most about the church at Colossae?

Do you think those dangers affect us today too?

What things do you think you should decide to get rid of? Which things should you decide to clothe yourself with today?

Lesson 39 > Colossians

What about Jesus?

Read the song that Paul includes in the text of Colossians 1:15—20.

Decide

I decide to clothe myself in Jesus, and strip myself of everything that is left over, watching out for the dangers that suggest wrong ideas about what christianity is.

 To pray is a good decision. Take time to pray before dismissal.

 Remember to download the daily readings, For Depth and Applications, from www.e625.com/lessons.

Lesson 40 > PHILEMON

The freedom of Onesimus

Behind this epistle lies a story worthy of a Hollywood script. If we do not know the story, we will miss most of this letter's teachings, and that is why we will study the characters—who perhaps appear in other parts of Scripture. there is much to learn from this short epistle that has only twenty—five verses. Condensed in those verses many teachings are relevant for us today.

Many people will fail us, and we will have to decide whether to hold a grudge, or forgive and become free. Although Onesimus—the letter's protagonist—made bad decisions in the past, God transformed him. And at the time Paul writes the epistle, he honors his name (Onesimus means "useful").

Although in the past he was someone who was not useful, when transformed by God he became someone valuable.

Read the entire letter to Philemon. Listen to the audio.

Download the letter to Philemon from www.e625.com/lessons.

Who does Onesimus seem to be? And Philemon? How did Paul and Onesimus meet?

We will use the structure of the text to delve into the context and discover the fascinating story behind this short epistle.

Encourage the teens to take notes, underline the text with different colors, and put whatever they feel is necessary in the margin to express meaning.

Division and structure

Salutation (vw. 1—3)
Let's look at the context.
Who is Onesimus?

Actually, we have already met this character although perhaps we did not realize it. He appears in Colossians 4:7—9 (read this passage).

Lesson 40 > Philemon

Onesimus is one of the people taking the letter to the Colossians from Rome, along with Tychicus. So Paul sent not only the letter to the church in Colossae, that we saw the previous week; there was also a personal epistle to Philemon, the owner of the house where the church met, to his wife Apphia and to Archippus (probably his son). Paul writes this personal letter to the leadership of the church in Colossae.

The love and faith of Philemon (vv. 4—7)

According to these verses, what is Philemon's character like? What is he known for?

Philemon means affectionate or one who is kind.

Paul intercedes for Onesimus (vv. 8—22)

We get to the heart of the epistle, where Paul pulls out all his arsenal. Let's read from verse 8 through 16.

Who was Onesimus for Philemon?

Onesimus was a slave who had escaped and had gone to Rome, to hide in the capital.

At that time slavery was legal, there were millions of slaves who were bought and sold, and many of them were born as slaves in their families. It was a well institutionalized system, and if a slave ran away and was caught, his master could end his life. So, Onesimus fled as far as he could: to Rome. But for some strange reason or by divine providence, he met Paul in prison in Rome, and there he met the Lord (v. 10).

Legally Onesimus belonged to Philemon, and he was a prisoner of justice, so Paul sends him back to Colossae, but with this petition letter to Philemon. Paul does not appeal to his authority as an apostle, but pleads from the heart, with an endearing attitude.

Where in the text do we see this attitude?

He begs Philemon to forgive Onesimus and to receive him not as a slave but as a brother and a person.

Why does the Gospel dignify people? What do you think God thinks of slavery?

Today there are still millions of slaves in our world, and as followers of Jesus we are called to eradicate this great evil.

From verse 17 through verse 22 Paul commits himself, because although forgiveness is based on love, someone still has to pay. Paul encourages Philemon to receive Onesimus as he'd receive him, and tells him that he himself will pay him back if Onesimus has stolen anything from him or has done him any harm. He commits himself to this in this letter by writing it in his own handwriting.

What does this attitude remind you of?

This is how Jesus saves us. He finds us like the prodigal son, restores us, and dignifies us so we are longer be slaves but brothers. His love paid the debt that we had.

This letter is a story that condenses the Gospel in an incredible way and illustrates biblical principles in a practical way.

What do you think of this phrase?

"God's plan is not to change the system at first, but to change people so they change the system."

What should we change in ourselves to then change the system today?

Greetings and final blessing (vv. 23—25)
At the end of the text, Paul reminds us that he is still in prison—although with the hope of getting out—and names some old acquaintances of ours, including Mark and Luke.

Do you know who they are?

That's right! Some of the writers of the Gospels that bear their names. They were part of Paul's inner circle.

Important questions, important decisions

What have we learned today from the letter to Philemon?
How do you think the story ended?

Who are you in this story? Onesimus, who knows that he's been forgiven? Paul, who intercedes for his brother? Philemon, who must forgive betrayal?

Each of us are one of them, and we must learn to decide wisely, whoever we are.

What about Jesus?

Jesus is the one who paid our debt, who freed us from slavery, gave us freedom, and made us Onesimus: useful for his kingdom despite our past.

Decide

I decide to be useful to others and serve them, not because I am their slave but because Jesus has set me free to love them.

 To pray is a good decision. Take time to pray before dismissal.

 Remember to download the daily readings, For Depth and Applications, from www.e625.com/lessons.

Lesson 41 > 1ST TIMOTHY AND TITUS

Letters to disciples in mission

There are some epistles of Paul known as the pastoral letters, which were addressed not to a church but to specific individuals who were in charge of communities of faith, specifically Timothy and Titus. These letters are very similar in content. If there had been photocopiers at that time, Paul would have used them, and yet each of the letters has its unique characteristics.

Who were Timothy and Titus?

Timothy

Timothy appears in many places in the book of Acts (17:14—15; 18:5; 19:22; 20:4) and is also mentioned in other letters of Paul (Rom. 16:21; 1 Cor. 4:17; 16:10; 2 Cor. 1:1; Philem 2:19; Col. 1:1; 1 Thes. 1:1; 3:2, 6; 2 Thes. 1:1; Philem 1).

In fact, Timothy co-authored some of Paul's epistles.

Here you can emphasize how the books of the New Testament are related to each other, and how it is necessary to study them as a whole to understand the stories and texts that are part of it. Decide if you want them to read the above texts to get an overview of the person of Timothy, or you can ask the group to study the letter during the session to expand their knowledge.

Timothy's mother was a Christian and his father was of pagan origin. Paul met him in Lystra when he was a twenty-year-old young man, and Timothy was Paul's companion on some of his missionary trips. Later, the young disciple of Paul was sent to Asia Minor to watch over some faith communities so that they would not be led astray by false, harmful, and destructive teachings.

Timothy resided in Ephesus, from where he practiced his ministry. And that's where this letter (1 Timothy) was sent, giving instructions to a young leader with great responsibilities.

Titus

Titus is mentioned in three of Paul's letters (2 Cor. 2:13; 7:6, 7, 13, 14; 8:6, 16, 23; 12:18; Gal. 2:1—3; and 2 Tim. 4:10).

Lesson 41 > 1st Timothy and Titus

In Acts Titus does not appear explicitly, but we know that he was a companion of Paul on his trip to Jerusalem, when the assembly of Acts 15 took place.

Some time later, Paul put Titus in charge of some missions—not easy ones—like establishing order in the Corinthian church (do you remember the problems of that church?), and organizing the life of the Christian community on the island of Crete. That is where this personal letter from the apostle Paul to Titus comes in, while he was in Crete, to provide Titus with encouragement and support.

Again, you can provide the group with the texts found in this Titus session.

Form two teams to study Timothy and Titus separately, each one with its structure and the texts that they must study in order to answer the questions posed. Once the study is finished, share it with the rest of the group by revealing the meaning of the letter, its teaching, etc.

Supervise the task of the two groups with some tips from us. Remember that you must have studied the lesson first.

Download sheets 1 and 2 at www.e625.com/lessons.

Division and structure

1 TIMOTHY

Ministry reminders (1:1—20)
Why did Paul send Timothy to Ephesus?

What problems do you think they had in those communities (1:3—7)?

Remember the phone: we only know this side of the conversation, but we can tell what was happening on the other side based on the text.

What does Paul remind Timothy of? What is Paul's attitude, even though he is already an experienced apostle (1:12—16)?

God's grace is Paul's foundation: he never forgets how much God has forgiven him.

Ministry standards (2:1—3:16)
What priority does Paul encourage Timothy to have in his spiritual life (2:1, 8)?

Prayer as a priority in our spiritual life.

When you talk about this point, take the opportunity to ask them: is prayer our priority in our service to God, or are there other things that we put ahead of it?

What are the requirements that we must have in order to serve God? Make a list combining 3:2—7 and 3:8—11.

It might be a good idea to make them think about whether we meet those criteria (obviously they're not married yet, but the context is understood). Perhaps we should make decisions to change some attitudes, right?

Ministry responsibilities (4:1—6:21)
Although Timothy is young, Paul encourages him to be an example.

In what practical ways should Timothy be an example (4:11—16)?

Encourage them to be as practical and specific as possible in this section.

What particular problem existed in that community (5:3—16)?

There was an issue with their treatment of widows. Some were idle, some were not being treated well, some were gossipy. Timothy had to take care of this situation, which at that time was precarious, because a widow had lost her financial support, and the church had to take care of her. But there were some people who took advantage of the situation. Timothy, with the right attitude, had to fix the problem.

What other problem did Timothy have to face (6:3—10)?

What's Paul's advice (6:11—14, 20—21)?

Could you make a one—paragraph summary explaining what Paul's first epistle to Timothy consists of? Use the different problems that appear and look at how Paul advises him, and determine what you think the purpose of the letter is.

What practical application does this letter have for us today?

TITUS
Greeting (1:1—4)
Requirements of elders and bishops (1:5—16)

Lesson 41 > 1st Timothy and Titus

Why did Paul send Titus to the island of Crete?

What characteristics should the leaders that are chosen have?

What problem do you think is occurring (1:10—11)?

How does Paul define Cretans (1:12)?

Let them know that Paul is not the author of that phrase here. It comes from a Cretan poet named Epimenides, who wrote it in the sixth century B.C.

Sound doctrine (2:1—15)

What does Paul advise Titus in this situation?

In 2:1 he speaks of "sound doctrine."

What is "sound doctrine" in this context?

The emphasis is that sound doctrine here has more to do with people's conduct in their home, in dealing with one another, and in living justly, rather than with an obsession over specific knowledge.

Justified by grace (3:1—11)

Based on the character of the Cretans, what else does Paul encourage Titus to help them remember (3:1—7)?

Toward the end of the letter Paul returns to emphasizing grace, because he appeared to be emphasizing works. But we should remember that it's grace that prompts us to do good works.

What things does Paul tell Titus that he should avoid? What last advice does he give him (3:8—10)?

Can we figure out what problems Crete had, based on these texts?

Epilogue (3:12—15)

What can we infer from this last section? Did Paul work alone? Why?

The emphasis is to see that Paul worked with a team and, although it's not always seen clearly in the New Testament, teamwork was fundamental to the spread of the Gospel.

 Can you make a one—paragraph summary explaining Paul's epistle to Titus? Discuss the different problems that are referenced, Paul's advice, and what you see as the purpose of the letter.

 What practical application does this letter have for us today?

Important questions, important decisions

 Do we see any similarities in the two letters? What are they?

What has caught your attention the most about these epistles?

Do you think it was necessary to write these letters? Why?

 What do you think was the most difficult issue that Timothy and Titus had to face?

What about Jesus?

Jesus is the one who sends us on the mission. He is the center of our message, reminding us that it is his grace that saves us, not ourselve. He is the one who gives us grace, mercy and peace in the midst of our problems.

Decide

I decide to faithfully fulfill the mission that God has entrusted to me, in the context in which God has placed me, fulfilling his purpose and helping others to be faithful to God's Word.

 To pray is a good decision. Take time to pray before dismissal.

 Remember to download the daily readings, For Depth and Applications, from www.e625.com/lessons.

Lesson 42 > 2ND TIMOTHY

Paul's testament

What would your last words be if you knew that your end was near? What would your last tweet or post on Facebook be? What photo would you put on Instagram? In the first century there was none of that, but at the end of his days Paul wrote Timothy his last words, full of passion, content, fervor and mission. This letter would be a compass in the decision—making process of Timothy, his "beloved son"... and it can also be ours.

Paul wrote his last epistle from prison (we can place it during the time of Nero, around 66—67). It is a particularly dramatic letter; Paul knows that his end is near, so he pours out his wisdom to Timothy, his beloved son, in this spiritual testament that can also guide us in our day-to-day life.

In this session it is important that you have your Bibles at hand to follow the text and its structure, which we will look at from a bird's-eye view.

Division and structure

Greetings (1:1—2)

Testifying about Christ (1:3—18)

Both Timothy's grandmother and mother (1:3—5) taught him the Word of God. All of us are heirs to what other people have done for us.

But now it's up to us (1:6—8).

What does Paul encourage Timothy to do? When do you think we need those words for ourselves?

The Gospel is a Gospel of grace, it drives us to follow Jesus and serve him and to be able to overcome any trial (that's why Paul reminds of us that in 1:11—12).

A good soldier of Jesus Christ (2:1—13)

Paul encourages Timothy to continue to be a witness, and he is also speaking to us today (2:1—2). We must teach others, so that they in turn teach others, and so on until the end.

How should we behave? In 2:4—7, Paul uses three images.

Download at www.e625.com/lessons the complementary material for this section.

Let us be soldiers, athletes and laborers.

What characteristic do we learn from each of them?

Don't get entangled, fight legitimately, don't cheat, and make an effort to work hard.

How do we apply those principles in our lives today?

For example, are there too many things in our lives that get in the way of following Jesus? Are we doing things that we know are wrong? Are we cheating ourselves? Are we being lazy, unmotivated, or fickle in following Jesus?

Paul, in 2:8—13, speaks of his situation but with hope ("the word of God is not imprisoned") and includes, as is his custom, a poem or song.

An approved worker (2:14—26)
"Tips for making good decisions": Divide into groups of three or four adolescents. Read this text and make a list of tips for making good decisions and to be "approved." Make two lists, titled What should we do? and What should we avoid?

Characteristics of men in the last days (3:1—17)
In 3:1—9, Paul, reaching the end of his days, foresees what people will be like in the future, and diagnoses them.

What does he say about these people?

Have them read that section aloud.

Is this how people are today? Dsicuss this question to arrive at the answers.
"But you…". We must accept this "but" for ourselves.

Let's read 3:14—16.
That is exactly what we want from these lessons. The Word of God can make us

wise to be active in the midst of this reality. Learning from the Word is what will help us make better decisions, as we have been learning throughout this study.

Preach the word (4:1—8)
But not only do you have to know the word, you also have to share it. It's not just for you!

Let's read 4:6—8. Here, Paul acknowledges that he is nearing his end.

With what attitude does he face it?

How would you like to face the end of your story?

Personal instructions (4:9—18)
Here Paul mentions some important people who collaborated with him (for example, two of the evangelists: Luke and Mark). The legacy that Paul left behind was amazing. May our life also be like this!
— Epilogue (4:19—22)

Reserve some time for the last dynamic (perhaps you can present it before beginning the lesson). Manage the time so that they can spend at least ten or fifteen minutes on this last activity.

Write the last thing you would want to say to the people around you (it could be to this group of teenagers, or to family, friends, etc.).

Do it yourself, or prepare it during the week to read in front of your group. It can be an emotional and meaningful moment for them. Remember that we are not just transmitting information, but making disciples of Jesus.

Important questions, important decisions

Why do we call 2 Timothy "Paul's testament"?

What do you think was the inheritance he left behind?

How does this letter help us in our decision making?

What about Jesus?

Jesus is Paul's reason for living: this is his legacy. His message is the most important treasure that he delivers to his "son" Timothy.

Decide

I decide to accept the legacy that Paul, Timothy and many other disciples of Jesus accepted, and that the legacy that I will leave on this earth will be about the kingdom of God and his justice.

 To pray is a good decision. Take time to pray before dismissal.

 Remember to download the daily readings, For Depth and Applications, from www.e625.com/lessons.

Lesson 43 > 1ST PETER

Heart of a pastor

In this letter written by Peter we see a huge pastoral heart. God had dealt a lot with Peter, that impulsive fisherman who appears in the Gospels.

He writes from Rome—although in a metaphorical sense he calls it "Babylon"—and the letter is addressed to various communities of believers scattered throughout territories in Pontus, Galatia, Cappadocia, Asia, and Bithynia.

Download at www.e625.com/lessons the complementary material for this section.

In 5:12 Peter tells us that he writes this letter through Silvanuw (the Latin form of the name Silas), a collaborator of Paul who appears elsewhere (Acts 15:22; 18:5; 2 Cor. 1:19; 1 Thess. 1:1, and 2 Thess. 1:1). It is written at a high level of Greek. Apparently, Silas helped Peter write it.

The purpose of the letter is to encourage its recipients to maintain—in the midst of persecution, problems and heartbreaks—a clean conduct, worthy of those who profess faith in Jesus. But the entire epistle is bathed in a pastoral attitude that exhorts them to continue moving forward.

 Pastoral advice

 Imagine that you are Peter. What advice would you give to a church in the following circumstance?

 Name each circumstance and have the teens answer out loud what their advice would be.

- A church that is discouraged because people are leaving.

- A church that, due to persecution, has no place to congregate and must take precautionary measures.

- A large, very successful church, but one that is neglecting its Christian behavior.

- A church in which there are arguments among the brethren, and that is not preaching the Gospel.

In this epistle we will see a structure which, as usual, begins with a theological foundation of what God has done and the identity he has given us. Then comes a theoretical part that supports what we must do, which will be the practical part that results from the above. We will also see throughout the letter some of the circumstances that the recipients were dealing with.

Download the diagram of the structure to be completed from www.e625.com/lessons.

Division and structure

Prologue (1:1—12)
Who writes it? For whom? What circumstances are they experiencing?

Have the adolescents answer these questions on the diagram. You can expand on the last question later, because the text gives more information.

New life in Christ (1:13—2:10)
What has God done for us (1:13—25)?
What identity has God given us? Who are we now (2:4—10)?

Living stones (it's interesting that the author is called Peter, isn't it?), royal priesthood, holy nation, a people acquired by God.

God works first with our identity and then with what we do, because what we are determines our actions.

Duties of believers (2:11—4:6)
What specific things does Peter advise? Why should they do them?

Have them choose one of these sections (you can tell them which one to focus on, and then they can share it with the rest of the group): 2:11—17; 2:18—25; 3:1—8; 3:9—17; 4:1—6.

The believers as the end approaches (4:7—19)

**What specific circumstance does this section describe?
How should the believers act?**
"The end of all things is near." The believers lived in the hope that the return of Jesus was near, and they were experiencing persecution, being attacked, suffering for being Christians, going through the "fire of being tested." Peter encourages them to help each other and to rejoice.

Do you know someone who is going through a similar situation? What would your advice be?

Specific advice (5:1—11)

What's his advice for leaders (5:1—4)?
What's his advice to young people (5:5—9)?
What does he teach us (5:10—11)?

He brings us back to what God has done and continues to do.

Epilogue (5:12—14)

Is there any significant information?

Silvanus and Marcos (the one from the Gospel) appear. Rome is referred to as Babylon.

Important questions, important decisions

What do you think is the main teaching of 1 Peter?

How does it help us in our decisions?

Can we identify in any way with the first recipients of this epistle?

How is it similar to Paul's letters? How is it different?

Remember that this is not just a one—way transmission of information, as is the case with Peter. We are making disciples of Jesus and pastoring.

What about Jesus?

Jesus is the living stone, rejected by men but chosen and precious to God, the cornerstone supporting the building that is us, the church.

Decide

I decide not to get discouraged in the midst of my circumstances and to remember my identity in Christ in order to act wisely in the midst of my trials.

The whole BIBLE in a year — HIGH SCHOOL

 To pray is a good decision. Take time to pray before dismissal.

 Remember to download the daily readings, For Depth and Applications, from www.e625.com/lessons.

Lesson 44 > 2ND PETER

This week and next we will see how 2 Peter and Jude are related letters. Some say that 2 Peter is an amplification of Jude, and others that Jude is a summary letter of 2 Peter (at least of chapter 2).

In any case, although their themes are very similar, and they often use the same examples, each has its own unique qualities. We can learn specific things from 2 Peter that do not appear in Jude, and vice versa.

While in 1 Peter the danger came mainly from outside the church. In this epistle Peter will warn us against the infiltration of erroneous doctrines and destructive attitudes (a very bad combination) within the church, because the greatest dangers to the church do not come from the outside but from within.

What dangers can the church suffer from the outside? And from within?

Which do you think are more dangerous? Why?

In this letter there are many allusions to the Old Testament, so it is important to have a comprehensive knowledge of Scripture.

Again, this letter is intended to strengthen the faith and the hope of believers.

We will form two large groups, to study chapters 1 and 3 of the letter of 2 Peter. At the end of the lesson, each group will share with the other what they have observed. To do this, we must download the two worksheets.

Download worksheet 1 (2 Peter 1) and worksheet 2 (2 Peter 3) from www.e625.com/lessons.

Division and structure

Greeting (1:1—2)
The author, Peter, introduces himself, along with the wish that grace and peace will multiply in the lives of the recipients. He does not say to whom the letter is addressed, so we assume that it is for the believers of the different churches of the "diaspora."

Participants in the divine nature (1:3—15)

Eyewitnesses to the glory of Christ (1:16—21)

False prophets and teachers (2:1—22)

This chapter is very similar to the letter of Jude, so we will study it next week.

The day of the Lord will come (3:1—18)

WORKSHEET 1
Participants in the divine nature (1:3—15)
   (Read the full passage.)

What do we need to live as God commands?

(Context: 2 Peter 1:5—11)

What does he encourage us to add to our faith?

FAITH - GOOD CONDUCT - UNDERSTANDING - SELF CONTROL - PATIENCE - DEVOTION TO GOD - BROTHERLY AFFECTION - LOVE

Why should we decide to enter this process (v. 8)?

What happens if we don't try?

(Context: 2 Peter 1:12—15)

At what point in his life where does Peter find himself? How does he describe his body? Why?

Eyewitnesses to Christ's glory (1:16—21)
   (Read the full passage.)

Why is Peter so sure of what he says?

What does he say about Scripture?

How should we interpret it?

Lesson 44 > 2nd Peter

 That's what we're doing today: interpreting it together. We can see how Peter mentions all the Scriptures, the prophets, etc, to support his point. He also places himself as a witness of that Jesus experience that marked his identity: "You are my beloved Son," putting both the Old Testament and the New Testament as the Word of God.

Let us summarize chapter 1 to share with the others.

WORKSHEET 2
The day of the Lord will come (3:1—18)
   (Context: 2 Peter 3:1—2)

What is the purpose of this letter, and the previous one (1 Peter)?

   (Context: 2 Peter 3:3—9)

What problem are the recipients of this letter going through?

Apparently they were expecting that the Lord would come back soon, and the fact that he had not done so was a source of discouragement for them.

What advice does Peter give them?
What reason does Peter give them for why Jesus has not returned yet?

   (Context: 2 Peter 3:10—13)

Let's describe, according to these verses, the end of history.

If the end of history is like this, what does Peter invite us to do (vv. 11—12)?

The ultimate end will be a new heaven and a new earth (as also shown in Revelation, where justice will dwell).

   (Context: 2 Peter 3:14—16)

What should we strive for?

Who does Peter mention? Why? What does he call the letters of the person he mentions?

He mentions Paul, with whom earlier he had had some differences, but who he now considers a writer of nothing more and nothing less than the Scriptures!

(Context: 2 Peter 3:17—18)

How does this letter end?

Let's summarize chapter 3 in one paragraph to share with the others.

Chapter 2 talks about the danger of false teachers and how to protect ourselves from them. Let's keep this in mind as we interpret chapter 3. Mention it so we can understand the full meaning of the letter.

Let's share the two worksheets and draw conclusions.

Important questions, important decisions

What do you think is the main theme of 2 Peter?

How can we practice patience in our lives?

Do you think we are living at the end times? Why?

How does our way of living change if we know the end of history?

What about Jesus?

Jesus is the beloved Son of God who will return soon to give justice.

Decide

I decide to follow God's wisdom, to behave as God commands, so as not to be blind in the midst of the decisions I must make in life, adding to my faith concrete acts that will help me grow in him, until his return.

To pray is a good decision. Take time to pray before dismissal.

Remember to download the daily readings, For Depth and Applications, from www.e625.com/lessons.

Lesson 45 > JUDE

Important warnings

When we are in a vehicle and we see warning signs, we must be careful. They are there for our own good, so that we do not derail or suffer accidents, and so that we can make the right decisions in terms of the direction we are going, the speed we are traveling at, and what we must watch out for. That is what the letter of Jude is about.

It is important to warn us of the dangers of the Christian life, which already in the first century were worse than they are today (and they are still valid). In this lesson we will examine some of the dangers that Jude warns us about, and we will learn how to make good decisions in order to avoid them.

Who was Jude?

The one who writes this letter is not Jude the traitor. Jude was the brother of James, the author of the letter of James, who was a brother of Jesus. So Jude was also a brother of Jesus.

For this lesson we are going to go to the text and we are going to ask direct questions to find out the themes. Form groups of three or four people to work on the themes and then share them.

Download the worksheet from www.e625.com/lessons.

Division and structure

The main purpose of the letter is for us to be keepers of the faith, to be constant, to take care of the faith that was delivered to the saints, not to wait for the novelties, or let ourselves be deceived; not to dilute the message and turn our freedom into debauchery. Keep this in mind when guiding the adolescents.

Greeting (1—2)
(Read the mentioned verses.)

Who writes it? For whom?

False doctrines and teachers (3—16)
(Read verses 3 and 4.)

❓ What decision does he encourage them to make?

❓ What problem do they have in the community?

(Read verses 5 through 11.)

❓ What are the three dangers that he warns us about in verse 11?

The three dangers: envy (Cain), personal interest (Balaam) and rebellion (Korah).
(Read verses 12 and 13.)

❓ What are these people doing?

(Read verses 14 through 16.)

❓ What else do they do?

Admonition and exhortation (17—23)

(Read the mentioned verses.)

❓ What practical advice does Jude give to guard us against these dangers?

❓ How can we live in a practical manner (vv. 22 and 23)?

Doxology (24—25)
(Read verses 5 through 11.)

Encourage the teens to share their answers, to add the dangers they see Jude exposing, and encourage discussion and dialogue about whether we may be experiencing similar dangers today. You can use the questions in the following section or others. There are some difficult passages that they may not understand, such as the one that refers to Enoch, but due to the length of this lesson, we believe that it is not advisable to address them.

Important questions, important decisions

❓ How would you summarize the theme of this letter?

Lesson 45 > Jude

Do you think we can be exposed to these dangers today? How?

What choices can we make to guard against these dangers?

Do you think this warning letter is important? Why?

How do you think this text can help you today?

What about Jesus?

Jesus is the one who keeps us so that we do not fall, the one who cleanses and protects us, our older brother!

Decide

I decide to guard myself from the dangers that are in my way—be they people or attitudes—and to allow Jesus to be the one who protects my life.

 To pray is a good decision. Take time to pray before dismissal.

 Remember to download the daily readings, For Depth and Applications, from www.e625.com/lessons.

Lesson 46 > HEBREWS

Jesus is more than everything else

There is no epistle more focused on the person of Jesus than Hebrews. The author is unknown, but due to its extraordinary content it earned its rightful place in the canon of Scripture. It is such a sublime text that its divine inspiration is undeniable. t is the most stylistically refined text of the entire New Testament. The summary would be that Jesus is superior to everything, to any religious system, any past history, any giant building, etc. Jesus is more than enough for us.

The recipients of the letter to the Hebrews were perhaps being tempted to look back at their surroundings, which seemed to have more power than the simple message that Jesus is everything. The author demonstrates the superiority of Jesus over anything, and shows that he is all we need to move forward in our Christian life.

What are things that might tempt us to leave the faith? Why?

How would you define what faith is?

Division and structure

- Prologue — God speaks through the Son (1:1—4)
- The Son, superior to the angels (1:5—2:18)
- The Son, superior to Moses (3:1—4:13)
- The Son, superior to the priesthood of Aaron (4:14—7:28)
- Jesus, mediator of a new covenant (8:1—10:18)
- Exhortation to faithfulness and trust (10:19—11:40)
- Eyes set on Jesus (12:1—29)
- Christian life (13:1—19)
- Epilogue (13:20—25)

WORKFLOW

In this lesson we will see the structure in different ways: at first you present it and then we do some dynamics for understanding, and finally we return to a closing presentation with the questions that we always ask in the lessons. This text is amazing!

Prologue — God speaks through the Son (1:1—4)

This is the presentation of the completed masterpiece. It is worth reading it and realizing that from the beginning it tells us that everything that comes after it will talk about Jesus, but it will be brilliantly done with numerous examples taken from the Old Testament.

As we have been teaching in all these lessons, the Bible has a common message from beginning to end, and Hebrews is an extraordinary example of this. We will see how the Old Testament enriches the person of Jesus and our trust in him.

We will see how in the text Jesus is compared to various things, always putting him above it or perfecting it. The author shows us that everything pointed to Jesus, and then encourages us to put our trust and faith in him and not turn back.

 For this, we will download the file for the teams and will study the structure of Hebrews according to the proposed scheme.

 Download sheet 1 (for this dynamic) and sheet 2 (for the next dynamic) from www.e625.com/lessons.

In teams of three or four people, they should complete the given diagram using the different sections of the text from Hebrews (we recommend that they have their physical Bibles to do this).

JESUS, THE SON

Section 1: The Son, superior to the angels (1:5—2:18)
Jesus, the high priest (2:17—18)
Why is he powerful to help us?

Section 2: The Son, superior to Moses (3:1—4:13)
The fulfillment of the day of rest (4:8—11)
What is the function of the Word of God (4:12—14)?

Section 3: The Son, superior to the priesthood of Aaron (4:14—7:28; highlight 5:10)
Jesus, the high priest (4:14—16)
Why can he empathize with us?

Section 4: Jesus, mediator of a new covenant (8:1—10:18; highlight 9:15)
What is the main point of all of Hebrews (8:1)?
What covenant does God make with us through Jesus? (10:15—17)

The whole BIBLE in a year for HIGH SCHOOL

Comment about the structure up to this point. This would be roughly the theoretical part or the foundation that the author wants to expose.

How would you summarize the letter to the Hebrews so far?

They should answer out loud (here we should be at about the middle of the session).

Exhortation to faithfulness and trust (10:19—11:40)

From here on the author asks us for an answer.

What should we do, in a practical way, if Jesus is what we have seen in all the previous sections (10:19—24)?

Examples of faith from the Old Testament

Using Hebrews 11 as a base, have them choose four characters from those that appear in the text, and talk about what each received by faith in God. Have them complete the sheet and answer the questions. They can work in the same groups they had before.

Use the second downloaded sheet

How would you define in your own words what faith or trust in God is?
Characters (choose three characters from Hebrews 11, and answer the questions):
What did they do? In which other book of the Bible do they appear?

Let's read Hebrews 11:33—40.

What do we learn from this text?
The idea is to show them the two faces of the faith. Trusting in God does not mean that everything will go well for us. Our decisions should be based on our faith in God, but that does not mean that everything will always be rosy. We see examples in this text of people who gave their lives for their faith in God. Are we willing to do it?

Have them share with the rest of the group some of the characters they have put on the sheet. Manage the time that you have left in the class.

Lesson 46 > Hebrews

Eyes set on Jesus (12:1—29)

Reading 12:1—2 and after everything we've seen, the author turns our attention back to the central theme: Jesus. He encourages us to continue and not throw in the towel. In the midst of any circumstance, let's look at him; it's the best decision we can make. If we stop looking at him, we can end up like Peter when he got out of the boat, and circumstances will make us sink. Let's not look at the storm, nor the waves nor the winds. Let us always look at him and keep going.

Christian life (13:1—19)

Here we find some very practical and concrete tips.
(You can share some of them if there is time, like 13:2, 5, 7, 15, 17, 18.)

Epilogue (13:20—25)

The letter ends with a blessing and greetings.

Important questions, important decisions

How would you summarize the theme of Hebrews?
What has caught your attention the most?
How does this help you in your day-to-day life?

What about Jesus?

Jesus is the ultimate high priest. He is God's revelation through whom he speaks to us. He is superior to everything, and we do not need anything else to know God and live life fully. He is the author and finisher of our faith.

Decide

I decide to place Jesus in the place that he deserves to be in my life, above everything, in the center of everything. I will not doubt him, nor put my trust in myself or in other things that can distract me from his path for me, because he is superior to everything.

To pray is a good decision. Take time to pray before dismissal.

Remember to download the daily readings, For Depth and Applications, from www.e625.com/lessons.

Lesson 47 › 1ST JOHN

John, the apostle of love, left us this incredible epistle so that we do not forget what is essential. Sometimes we add many ideas to the Gospel, many projects and initiatives; we add concepts that can be good, but that can also make us forget the essence, the central point of our message. John wants to bring it back through this letter, and he will make us focus on the most important commandments, on the DNA of Jesus. This first letter is the beginning of a trilogy, but the other two are much shorter and will deal directly with the specific issues for which they were written.

What is God like?

The idea is to look at what people think God is like, to lead adolescents to the concept that "God is love" as the main idea.

In this case, 1 John digs much deeper into the principles that Jesus taught. It is a letter that has inspired many believers to continue believing in the truth that 1 John 4:8 proclaims: "God is love."

We will see how in this letter, which appears to be more like a theological discourse than a letter since it doesn't mention either the author or the addressee and has no greetings or farewells, John will deal with various topics from different angles, repeating some ideas that he considers fundamental. We will also deduce that this letter is a response to some problems that were arising with what he calls "the antichrists." One of the most dangerous things to attack faith is a lack of unity and a lack of communion with each other. Likewise, one of the things that gives evidence of God's work in our lives is the love we have for one another.

First John is a text filled with tenderness, using words like "little children" and "beloved" but also one that teaches us very important and firm truths for the proper development of our faith.

When there is an argument between us, how do we handle it (for example, a fight with a friend or a disagreement with someone)? How should we resolve our conflicts?

What do our reactions to others say about our faith in God? What are the best decisions we can make when there is conflict between us?

Lesson 47 > 1st John

We will emphasize that personal relationships are important for spirituality (1 John 2:9—11).

To study the structure of 1 John we will make three groups to observe the three thematic developments into which the letter is divided. Thus we will see its main themes and what John wants us to learn. Each group will work separately with each file, answering the questions that arise.

Download the three sheets at www.e625.com/lessons.

Here we describe the general structure. We will see the concepts that are repeated in the three central sections.

Division and structure

- *Prologue (1:1—4)*
- *First thematic development (1:5—2:29)*
- *Second thematic development (3:1—4:6)*
- *Third thematic development (4:7—5:12)*
- *Epilogue (5:13—21)*

Sheet 1
First thematic development (1:5—2:29)

In 1:5—10

What is the main idea?

How is the relationship "with one another" associated here with spirituality?

In 2:1—11

What is the main idea?

How is the relationship "with one another" associated here with spirituality?

In 2:12—17

What advice do we find?

In 2:18—29, what is the problem that John denounces?

What advice does he give them? What decisions must they make?

Let's summarize in one paragraph what all this thematic development tells us, and what practical things it encourages us to do. Then we will share it with the other groups.

Sheet 2
Second thematic development (3:1—4:6)

In 3:1—12

What does it say about sin?

How is the relationship "with one another" associated here with spirituality?

In 3:13—24

What is the subject matter?

How is the relationship "with one another" associated here with spirituality?

In 4:1—6

What is the problem that John denounces?

What advice does he give them? What decisions must they make?

Let's summarize in one paragraph what all this thematic development tells us, and what practical things it encourages us to do. Then we will share it with the other groups.

Sheet 3
Third thematic development (4:7—5:12)

In 4:7—21

What is the subject matter?

How is the relationship "with one another" associated here with spirituality?
In 5:1—11

What does John say about Jesus?

Why do you think John insists so much on loving our brothers? Do you think there might be a problem that he wants to address for the recipients of the letter?

Let's summarize in one paragraph what all this thematic development tells us, and what practical things it encourages us to do. Then we will share it with the other groups.

At the end of the exercise—to which they could dedicate about twenty minutes—they must share with the rest of the adolescents the conclusions they have reached.

What conclusions does this exercise lead us to? Do you see similarities in the different sections? What are they?

Why does John repeat the concepts? What do you think is his intention?

In this letter we see that loving our neighbor is crucial, and that individualistic spirituality does not fit with what John is teaching. In all three sections, he emphasizes that love for God and love for one's brother are closely related.

We must anchor this concept well in this lesson. It is the intention of John and the emphasis throughout the text.

The epistle ends by telling us why he wrote it (read 1 John 5:13).

What is that purpose?

Important questions, important decisions

What decisions must we make regarding our spirituality according to this epistle?

Do you think there is something you must correct to fulfill what this letter teaches?

What has caught your attention the most from this epistle?

Do you see differences in style and structure compared to Paul's letters? What are they?

What about Jesus?

God is love, and Jesus (and what he did for us) is the greatest expression of that love.

Decide

I decide to live a spirituality in which others share an active part, where I live not only to love God but also to love others, watching out for those who promote selfishness. I decide to take care of my brethrem, and let them take care of me.

 To pray is a good decision. Take time to pray before dismissal.

 Remember to download the daily readings, For Depth and Applications, from www.e625.com/lessons.

Lesson 48 > 2ND AND 3RD JOHN

Short but effective letters

We now find two very short letters from John, the elder, someone well known in the churches. His emphasis is placed as always on love, which is the central axis of the message. In these epistles he launches very specific ideas into specific situations, always based on the essence of the Gospel. We learn not to lose sight of Jesus' teaching in the midst of our life in community.

Division and structure

Form two teams, one for each letter. Work on the text. At the end of the lesson share the conclusions between the two groups.

Download complementary material for this section at www.e625.com/lessons.

Remember to supervise their work and encourage them. and if you see that they are blocked, guide them in the study and remind them that we are working in an environment of trust to grow in our biblical knowledge.

2 JOHN

(Read 2 John in full.)

Greeting (vv. 1—3)

To whom is the letter addressed?

To God's chosen community, the church, and its members.

Walking in truth and love (vv. 4—6)

What two concepts does John present as key? Why?

What relationship is there between these two concepts?

The whole BIBLE in a year for HIGH SCHOOL

If you have a blackboard, you can draw a diagram explaining the connection that this text presents between truth (the commandments) and love, a circular relationship expressed in verse 6.

The best decisions are based on these two concepts: truth and love.

One without the other can be very dangerous. There are people who "with the truth up front" hurt people, and others who seem to use love as an excuse to say nothing, or base their love only on good feelings but not on concrete actions.

To love is a verb, it implies action, and it must be based not on chimera but on reality, on the truth.

Answer to the impostors (vv. 7—11)

What dangers lie in wait for this church? How should they avoid them?

The incarnation of Jesus is fundamental in the life of the Christian. God loved us based on the truth, in a real way, not just as a fantasy. Here we see how the doctrine of gnosticism—which we have seen in other lessons—also was stalking this church; it was based on theory, but without the presence of real love.

Do you think we face that danger today? In what ways?

Final greeting (vv. 12—13)
What do we learn from this conclusion?

There are many things that John needed to say face-to-face, not just in writing. Nothing can replace a personal meeting. In the letter he wrote what's fundamental, what's key, but there were other things to deal with. Not everything that happened in the early church is in the Bible!

Let's summarize the letter in a short paragraph.

3 JOHN

Greetings to Gaius (vv. 1—4)

To whom is the letter addressed? Perhaps it is the same Gaius who appears in the following texts. Let's see if it makes sense. Let's read Romans 16:23; Acts 19:29; 1 Corinthians 1:14, and then draw conclusions about who he was.

Lesson 48 > 2nd and 3rd John

What characteristics can we take from this greeting to find out what Gaius was like?

Gaius' conduct (vv. 5—8)

Make a list of the characteristics that John praises about Gayo in this section.

Hospitable, loving, welcoming, willing to take the initiative to serve others even if he doesn't know them, not selective, cooperative.

Diotrephes' opposition (vv. 9—10)

List the characteristics of Diotrephes.

He wants to be first, he is not hospitable, he speaks bad words, he is an authoritarian.

Here we see two examples: a good example and a counterexample, from which we learn how to act and how not to act.

Demetrius' good testimony (vv. 11—12)

What advice does John give in this section?

Who could Demetrius be?
It is possible that he was the bearer of the letter, the one they should welcome. Perhaps John expects Gaius to welcome him—and not Diotrephes—so the letter makes more sense, right?

Final greeting (vv. 13—14)

Let's summarize the letter in a short paragraph.

They are very similar endings. After the presentation of each letter, ask the following questions to the whole group.

Important questions, important decisions

What do these two epistles have in common?

What do we learn from them?

Which one do you like more? Why?

What about Jesus?

Jesus is truth and love. He is the one who teaches us to love one another as the nucleus of our community life.

Decide

I decide to live in the truth and according to God, as expressed in a life in community, being hospitable and practicing love in a real and authentic way.

 To pray is a good decision. Take time to pray before dismissal.

 Remember to download the daily readings, For Depth and Applications, from www.e625.com/lessons.

Lesson 49 > REVELATION

The last book: epistle, prophesy and revelation. A masterpiece!

In Greek, *apokalypsis* means revelation. This is the first word that appears in this text. It was written by none other than John, and it is an extraordinary book. Revelation presents the Gospel in creative ways, aimed at seven churches that were experiencing a variety of circumstances—from external persecution to internal despair—but it also aims much further than its own time.

From the hope of the resurrection it points to a glorious future where all God's promises will be fulfilled. It is based on that future that believers must live their lives and make wise decisions, while knowing how it all ends.

Apocalyptic literature is not exclusive to this book. It was a well-known style used under political oppression, using creative images to speak of their present situation, but in codes that only the recipients could understand. Thus, under the Roman Empire, it was common to find this type of text.

But this masterpiece is not just an apocalyptic book; it is also prophetic and it is also an epistle. And of course, it is a book that speaks of the Gospel from beginning to end, with the great protagonist being Jesus, the one who was, who is, and who is to come.

When you hear the word "apocalypse" what is the first thing that comes to your mind?

We must remember that this book was written for believers, not to instill fear in them but quite the opposite, to give them hope in the one who will return and bring justice.

We don't want this session to turn into a "Christian tabloid" filled with conjecture about Jesus' second coming. The central message is the hope that this book evokes. In times of difficulty it has been an anchor and a support to Christians always and everywhere.

Division and structure

- Prologue (1:1—8)
- The Son of Man and the churches (1:9—20)
- Letter to the seven churches (2:1—3:22)

 Make seven groups of two or three people. If there are not enough people in the group to cover the seven letters make teams of two until you reach three or four churches, and you as the leader can briefly explain the others.

Everyone will answer the following questions, spending about ten or fifteen minutes reading, studying the letter and answering the questions. Then they will present to the other groups the situation that church is in, what God tells it, and the decisions that they must make.

 Download the letters to the seven churches at www.e625.com/lessons.

Questions:

1- How does the one who writes it describe himself?
2- How does he describe the church? What strengths and weaknesses does it have? What are the positive and negative things?
3- What does he encourage them to do?
4- What will be the consequences for those victorious, the achievers?

Ephesus: 2:1—7
Smyrna: 2:8—11
Pergamum: 2:12—17
Thyatira: 2:18—29
Sardis: 3:1—6
Philadelphia: 3:7—13
Laodicea: 3:14—22

 **How can we apply these letters to our lives today? Do we see ourselves or others reflected in these letters? Why?**

The heavenly throne, the scroll and the Lamb (4:1—5:14)

After these letters, John presents us with a heavenly landscape, full of music, images of worship, a Lamb, a scroll and symbols that help us in a very graphic way to understand where history is taking us.

Lesson 49 > Revelation

Based on the time you have left, decide whether you want to go deeper into this passage or move on to the next section. If we read this text we realize that again there are many songs and poetry: 4:8, 11; 5:9, 10, 12, 13.

What does it tell us about what the end will be like?

We see that the great protagonist is always Jesus, who from Genesis through Revelation is the Lord of history, the Alpha and the Omega.

Map of the seven churches of Revelation
Download at www.e625.com/lessons complementary material for this section.

After this section, a series of images begin, many of them built around the number 7, which speak of the end of times in highly visual and evocative ways.

It is undoubtedly a difficult book to interpret. Much has been written about it and it is still very useful to us. To understand its images, we must have a good knowledge of the Old and New Testaments, of the historical context in which it was written, the intention of the author and many other things. In this session it will not be possible to cover everything, but the Bible is like that: it enlightens the simple but has wise men studying it for years. Isn't that cool?

Division and structure

- The seven seals (6:1—8:1)
- The seven trumpets (8:2—11:19)
- Seven signs (12:1—14:20)
- Seven bowls (15:1—19:5)
- The return of the King of kings (19:6—20:15)
- New heaven and new earth (21:1—22:5)
- Conclusion (22:6—21)

The end of all things, God's dream

Let's focus on the end of all history. . . all history (Revelation 21:1—22:21)

We must live in accordance with the end of the story to make good decisions. Many of us want to fulfill our own dreams, but have you considered fulfilling God's dreams?

Where is God pointing? What is his ultimate will?
We are going to read the end of history as God desires it, in Revelation 21:1—7.

What does this text tell us?

The story does not end with us leaving this planet but instead this earth becomes his heaven, his kingdom, and he will be among us.

We see that he will end pain, that he will make all things new, that there will be no death, no crying, no pain. This is God's dream.

But there is more!

Let's read Revelation 21:22—22:5.

What characteristics does the new Jerusalem have?

 Have them answer out loud.

We see that there will be no temple, because God is our temple; in him we live. It is a city that will have the tree of life.

 Where do you remember that tree from?

Exactly! From the garden of Eden. Now it is no longer in the middle of the garden, but in the middle of the city. Creation has advanced and we will dwell there; the Lord has restored all things, and from beginning to end everything makes sense.

Isn't it amazing how the Bible ends history in the same place where it started?

Gone is that tree of knowledge of good and evil, where each one made decisions independently of God. He makes us truly free and gives us access again to his presence, face-to-face.

 Knowing this ending, what can we decide to do today to fulfill God's dream? What is our part in his plan?

The ending is brilliant. Read Revelation 22:20—21.

Jesus is coming back, and our hope is based on that. We must continue to wait for it with faith and say like those early Christians: Come, Lord Jesus!

Lesson 49 > Revelation

Important questions, important decisions

What has surprised you the most about the book of Revelation?

Do you think the message to the seven churches is also for us today? Why?

How do you think the book of Revelation will be useful to you today in your daily decisions?

What about Jesus?

Jesus is the Lamb worthy of opening the seals, he is the Alpha and the Omega, he is the King of kings and Lord of lords, the Faithful and True, the one who was, the one who is and the one who is to come, the Almighty, the who keeps his promises and to whom all the history of humanity points, including our own history.

Decide

I decide to live in the hope that Revelation reveals to me in order to fulfill God's dream of bringing his kingdom to this earth, without being discouraged by the present circumstances, knowing that he is coming back.

To pray is a good decision. Take time to pray before dismissal.

Remember to download the daily readings, For Depth and Applications, from www.e625.com/lessons.

Lesson 50 › WHAT DOES GOD WANT US TO DO WITH OUR KNOWLEDGE OF THE BIBLE?

The Word of God was not created just to be studied. If it's all about knowing the structure of each book, its central idea, the author's purpose, its time and its context, but we do not live it in a practical way in our daily decision-making, then it is of little use. We are not blessed for being "hearers" only but "doers" of the Word. Knowing the Bible should lead us to live as the Bible teaches us.

Throughout this course we have traveled thousands of years of history, we have studied more than forty human authors and we saw a divine inspiration behind them that brought forth a message expressed in multiple histories.

What is the history or book that you liked the most during all these lessons?

In this lesson let's encourage teens to continue studying the Bible.
One proposal would be that they could take on the challenge of reading the whole Bible assisted by sometype of reading program within a year or two.

Look for a mobile app that may have this type of Bible reading program, like YouVersion. Let's learn to use these new technologies, wherever they are, to study the Word of God.

Download from www.e625.com/lessons a program for reading the Bible within one or two years.

Many times we will get discouraged or it will become difficult for us to keep reading, but having good discipline determines who we will become in the future.

The decisions we make today shape who we will be tomorrow. That is why it is important to have a good foundation to make our decisions.

Make teams of three people. Imagine that the Bible is like a novel that has a back cover. If you had to write the history of the Bible, what the central theme is, what would you write? Have each team write a back cover in two or three paragraphs, and then share it with the whole group.

This exercise should not last more than fifteen minutes.

Lesson 50 > What does God want us to do with the knowledge of the Bible?

How have these lessons helped you in your life and your decisions?

One thing that can be very helpful to us in order to continue the study of the Word is to not do it alone. A lone ranger is a dead ranger! Playing sports with others is always much better. If you so desire, plan to study the Bible together with other people from the group, as you are doing now. We can ask weekly how about their progress, or create a WhatsApp Bible reading group to remind us that we must keep going.

Can you think of other ideas to help each other persevere in Bible study?

This is a question for the whole group of teens, or you can have them discuss it in groups of three first and then share it. Remember, sometimes sharing it first in small groups helps to increase participation.

Do you think there is any danger in knowing the Bible too much?

The point of this question is that they delve into the idea that it's not helpful to just know many things and become proud of that. The Bible is not meant only to be studied, but also to be obeyed and put into practice. Let's not only fill our minds with a lot of knowledge. We must remember that knowledge can lead to vanity, but love edifies.

How would you like to continue with the Bible study? What would you like to know? What questions come to you after all these lessons?

What about Jesus?

Jesus is the Word of God made flesh. He is the perfect example of obedience to God, of blessing others, of knowing God's will to make the best decisions. "The Word became flesh," states John 1:14.

Decide

I decide to continue studying the Word of God and to apply it to every situation in my life in order to make good decisions.

Remember the commitment of reading the Bible in one year.

To pray is a good decision. Take time to pray before dismissal.

Remember to download the daily readings, For Depth and Applications, from www.e625.com/lessons.

NOTES

NOTES

NOTES

NOTES

NOTES

NOTES

NOTES

NOTES

NOTES

SOME QUESTIONS TO ANSWER:

WHO IS BEHIND THIS BOOK?

E625 is a team of pastors and servants from different countries, different denominations, different sizes and church styles who love Christ and the new generations.

WHAT IS E625.COM ABOUT?

Our passion is to help families and churches to find good materials and resources for the discipleship of new generations and that is why our website serves parents, pastors, teachers, and leaders 365 days a year through **www.e625.com** with free resources.

WHAT IS THE PREMIUM SERVICE?

In addition to free reflections and short materials, we have a service of lessons, series, research, online books, and audiovisual resources to facilitate your task. Your church can access them with a monthly subscription that allows all the leaders of a local church to share them as a team and make the necessary copies that they find pertinent to the different activities of the congregation or its families.

CAN I EQUIP MYSELF WITH YOU?

It would be a privilege to help you and with that objective, you can choose seminars at **www.e625.com** and academic courses at **www.institutoE625.com**.

Sign up for e625.com updates right now depending on your work arena: Pastors - Children - Preadolescents - Adolescents - College ministry.

LET'S LEARN TOGETHER!